Flamethrowers

Guardians of the game

Volume 1
Owl Nation Lacrosse

Based on the comic "Flame Boy" written by Brody Childs

J. Alan Childs

Savage, Minnesota, USA

ISBN-13: 978-1456300104
ISBN-10: 1456300105

Chapter illustrations
    by Bailey Childs & J. Alan Childs

Acknowledgements

I would like to thank those who helped inspire me to write and encouraged the concepts in this story.

Jenni Lorsung who motivated me to start writing.

Bailey for her photos at the zoo and many other places to make the chapter images.

Brody whose summer comic book project was the source of my inspiration.

A special thanks to Cindy Wilson who spent countless hours correcting punctuation and grammar and encouraged me to finish.

Flamethrowers

Guardians of the game

For Brody

Contents

Chapter		Page
1	Prairie Dogs	1
2	Legacy	15
3	Mariucci	23
4	Mine	36
5	Cave	48
6	Stick in the Stone	61
7	Guardians of the Game	71
8	Red Hawk Casino	81
9	Legend	92
10	Trapped	104
11	Red Rocks	116
12	Fireballs	126
13	Family and Friends	134
14	Balance of Power	142
15	Grounded	152
16	Breakout	166
17	Briggs' Revenge	174
18	Casey Falls	188
19	A Flamethrower Emerges	199
20	White Crane	219

1

Prairie Dogs

Kenny Conley stepped onto the ice again. *Another practice,* he thought to himself. How many times has he been inside this rink?

He was too young to remember his first time. It was two days after he was born that his mom stopped on her way home from the hospital to watch his oldest brother, Ryan, play a hockey game. Kenny's mom held him and cheered as Ryan played his first playoff game. It was an introduction to his family; and how he would be raised.

Kenny grew up living at his hometown rink in Brenton as his dad coached and his older brothers played hockey. Brenton is located on the Iron Range of Minnesota, home to large mining equipment and cold winters. Brenton was Minnesota hockey, having won several high school state championships and being home to many former college and professional hockey players.

Cody, Kenny's dad, had been born in Brenton and left to play hockey for the Gophers in Minneapolis. Then he was drafted to play professional hockey by the Minnesota North Stars. A true local boy done good.

Kenny was never asked if he wanted to play hockey; it was just expected. Ryan, his oldest brother, was now playing for the Gophers and Tommy, the middle brother, was playing for the Brenton high school hockey team. So naturally, everyone expected Kenny must *love* hockey and would the best player on his peewee team.

But Kenny was not the best player on his team. Kenny did not even like hockey. He had spent so much time in musty rinks, moldy locker rooms, and smelly car rides to and from his older brother's games. He'd grown to hate hockey. He wanted to be outside where he could breathe fresh air, not the exhaust of another run down

Zamboni that drove in endless circles scrapping the same rusty ice over and over.

Kenny's mom was the classic hockey mom, running the boys from practice to games, being the team manager, scheduling all the activities from the classic out-of-town tournaments to team parties. Hockey season in Brenton started with clinics in September and ran until March with the state tournament. Each day started and ended the same way, with school and then onto at least one rink every night. It was a blur to Kenny.

During the spring and summer his family ran hockey clinics. Kids would come from all over the country to be taught by his dad and now his older brothers. Kenny liked meeting kids from other states and seeing what they did. He also liked showing off some of the moves his brothers and dad taught him that seem to just amaze those kids.

But the hockey camps would go on for weeks during the summer and the kids would always vote to sleep at the rink and skate all night. Yep, another night at the rink, and another cold night during the short Minnesota summer.

Kenny had long blonde hair and blue eyes, all from a classic Norwegian heritage. Kenny had a scar on his right cheek where, as a little guy, he'd run through an open door on the boards at the ice rink and right into the Zamboni that was cleaning the ice.

"Kenny!" yelled out Casey, "You ready for the big game tomorrow? Eveleth will be looking for revenge for us beating them at their rink last month."

"Yah, sure" said Kenny in a slow and bored voice.

Casey was Kenny's best friend. She'd been playing hockey with Kenny since they were four. Casey was a classic tomboy and skated like the wind. She had long blonde hair that was always pulled back in a pony tail to fit under the helmet. And if she didn't have a helmet on, it was an old classic green and gold North Stars baseball cap.

In Brenton there wasn't much opportunity for girls' hockey teams to be formed, unless you joined a rainbow team of neighboring towns. Casey wanted nothing to do with anything called a 'rainbow' team; she wanted to represent Brenton and play with the boys she grew up with on the outdoor rinks.

Casey loved hockey and was jealous of Kenny's family, spending every chance she had at the Conley household to hang out with the boys and talk hockey. Unlike Kenny, Casey dreamed of playing hockey in college, then, maybe, in the NHL. Kenny wished she was the one born in his family and not him.

Practice finished up as usual with a speech about the upcoming game. Of course, this time it was the speech about the rival Eveleth Bears. Coach Harrington went on and on and on, talking about playing with pride and how rich the Brenton tradition was for peewee hockey and blah blah blah. Kenny had heard the speech so many times from his dad, brothers, and everyone who had coached him before.

The next evening, Kenny arrived at the rink as usual - over an hour early - to get ready for the game. Kenny could put his equipment on in his sleep, and had done that before; *five minutes max* he would think to himself. *Why do I have to be here inside for so long before the game when I could be doing something else?*

Casey ran up to Kenny. "Great, you're here! We can all go for a run to warm up."

Of course, a run was outside so Kenny didn't mind, but warm up? It was only 7 degrees out there!

Kenny was a captain on his team. They always made him captain because everyone assumed he knew everything about hockey because of his family. Kenny learned to hate being captain, always being in charge. *How come I can't just show up and have fun?* He always grumbled silently to himself.

Casey was a captain, too, and she was the organized one. And the one who loved the job. Kenny let her lead all the warm ups and give all the speeches to the team.

Early on, some boys didn't like that Casey played with the boys. But she earned her spot and made sure the boys knew she deserved to be there. In peewee tryouts, the first-year hockey players can lay on the full body checks but no one would hit her. They were scared to hit a girl. Then she removed that barrier by taking on Frank Larson, the biggest boy on the team. Frank took the puck from her on a rush and skated up the ice the other direction. From out of nowhere Casey took him out at the legs - a cheap shot - and Frank was thrown into the boards back-first, getting the wind knocked out of him.

Casey skated up to Frank and growled, "Nobody takes the puck from me."

Casey was not someone you wanted to play against. The local boys were glad she lived in their town.

The Bears skated onto the ice in their black and gold jerseys. The Brenton Prairie Dogs followed, dressed in their solid red jerseys trimmed in orange and yellow.

6

The teams warmed up for the traditional five minutes, and without introductions the teams took their benches. The starting players moved to the middle of the ice for the opening faceoff.

Casey would take the faceoff. She played a great center, being all over the ice, and Kenny was on the wing along with Brian. For defense, Fred of course started with his large size out there and Jeremy, a stringy tall kid. In goal was Paul, who had played with Kenny and Casey since they were mites.

Casey approached the faceoff circle. Her style was to always skate outside the circle right up until the referee dropped the puck. No jockeying for position or giving away what she was going to do...just zoom in right as the referee blew the whistle.

The whistle blew and Casey skated in. The puck dropped and Casey streamed by the other center into the zone. The Prairie Dogs set up in the offensive zone. Casey moved the puck over to Kenny. Kenny shot a pass to Brian, rotating in their triangle offense. Casey set up behind the net, making the defense move out of the front of the net. She moved the puck in front to Kenny who faked the shot and moved it over to Brian, who put the puck away. A play they have scored on dozens of times. Score 1-0 Prairie Dogs.

The Bears always seemed to start slow. As the game went on, they started pressing the Prairie Dogs and causing turnovers. By the end of the first period it was Prairie Dogs 1, Bears 2.

During the first period intermission, Casey urged her teammates. "Guys we gotta pick it up. They're beating us to the loose pucks!"

The coach agreed and spoke up. "We need to pressure them, remember how we beat them last month. Put lots of pressure on the player with the puck. Don't let them out of the zone without a fight!"

The second period continued and Casey was getting all sorts of pressure. She would get the puck to Kenny but he just couldn't put it home. Kenny had all sorts of skating skills and a talented stick but never felt he had to win the game. Give Kenny a great shot though, and he could rip it home. He just won't work for the shot.

Play continued. Casey, Kenny, and Brian jumped on the ice for their next shift. Casey lost the puck when the defensemen jabbed her in the ribs. *Cheap shot,* she thought. She chased down the defenseman and got her stick right in where she knows boys don't like it, pulled on her stick, and down the Bears defenseman went, barreling into the boards. TWEET!!! Penalty on Casey: two minutes for hooking.

The Bears went on the power play and set up in the offensive zone.

Casey yelled from the penalty box. "Don't get pulled out too far! Make them shoot from the outside!" Casey knew the penalty box well.

Inside the penalty box, it was an old tradition to write your number on the boards to show you had been there. Casey's number thirteen covered the boards. She had picked thirteen a long time ago when Brian took her favorite number, three, and she decided thirteen because it was going to be unlucky for the other team.

Just then a hard shot from the point came in on Paul. He noticed the middle was open and instead of gloving the puck and taking the faceoff in the zone, he dropped the puck in front of him and shot the puck down the ice, *HARD*. The Bear's goalie, seeing the puck going hard down the board, started to go behind his net to cut off the puck. But just as he turned, the puck took a wicked bounce and started heading right for the open net.

Everyone in the stands leapt to their feet and started screaming to get the goalie's attention. But the puck headed right into the net. Game tied, 2-2. Paul leapt in the air! He always wanted a goal, but being the goalie you didn't get many chances. Sure he had gotten assists before on long passes, but a goal was different. A goal was special for a goalie. The crowd went crazy and you could feel the team was lifted up. The second period came to an end and the team was excited.

"We got this game," Paul said. "How can they recover from me scoring on them?"

Coach Harrington cautioned them, "Don't let up, it's still tied. Now let's go take this!"

The third period saw the Prairie Dogs working hard and fast, controlling the puck. About the middle of the third period Paul again felt brave. He hit Kenny with a pass banking off the boards and Kenny, standing right on the blue line, caught the puck on a breakaway. Kenny's mind started racing; *okay forehand? Backhand? High shot, low shot? What should I do?*

Just as he decided *I'm going backhand upper left corner,* BAM! The Bears defensemen caught him from behind and with a shove Kenny went down. TWEET... the referee called out, "Tripping!" and put his arms, crossed, over his head. The Brenton hockey fans, who know their referee calls, cheered. Penalty shot!

But Kenny did not want a penalty shot. It meant he

10

was going to be out there all alone - no Casey, no Frank - just him and the Bear's goalie. Everyone watching. He felt sick.

Kenny knew that whether he scored or not, Dad and his brothers would be breaking down his every move from this shot for a month. What did Dad expect him to do? What would Ryan or Tommy do? What would Casey do? His mind raced, his body tensed up and he skated over to the bench as his coach motioned for him to come over.

Kenny waved his arm at the coach. "Coach you know anyone who was on the ice can take the shot."

Being around hockey, Kenny certainly knew his rules and especially if it meant getting him out of a situation. "Have Casey take it," Kenny begged.

The coach stepped down from the bench and leaned over the boards. "You know my rules Kenny. If you draw the penalty, it's your shot. Nobody else's."

Kenny lowered his head. He knew. But he tried. What would his mom say if he didn't take the shot? She'd be in the coach's face screaming, *"Why did you take that shot away from him?"*

Kenny knew this was his shot. His body was shaking. Sweat poured from under his helmet. He pushed his long-hockey-hair back under his helmet. Kenny skated out to the red line and met the referee. He heard the same instructions he'd heard before.

"Wait until the referee down by the goalie blows his whistle and then you can touch the puck. You get one shot, no rebound."

Kenny skated in a small circle to try and calm his nerves; he'd seen his brothers do it and thought this must help. Kenny heard the *tweet* and turned, skating at the puck. He touched the puck. It suddenly felt like a hundred pound weight, hard to push, and he knew this was not going to be good. *Why are they making me do this?*

He moved left and right, trying to make the goalie move. He hoped the goalie was more nervous than he was. As Kenny moved in, he saw his chance. The top left corner was open! He shot! BAM! He heard the puck hit the boards behind the net. He had missed the net. He felt sicker.

The Bear parents cheered and the Prairie Dog parents sat back down. Dejected. He felt their disappointment. The momentum had now switched to the Bears.

Kenny put his head down and skated to the bench. His shift was done for now. The Bears increased the pressure. The Bears started skating circles around the Prairie Dogs and taking shots left and right. Paul was doing a good job stopping them, but everyone could tell it was just a matter time if something didn't change.

Paul again saw an opening. This time Casey was sprinting up the ice. He skated out to get a clean pass off, only this time *whiff* he missed the puck. The net was wide open now and the puck was right at Paul's skates. A Bears forward dove at that puck, tipping it towards the net. Everyone watched as it slowly trickled across the goal line. Bears won 3-2.

The ride home was longer than normal. Dad was asking him, "Why don't you play harder, like your brothers?" "Why don't you practice more so when you get those chances you score?" One comment after another. Deflating Kenny. His brothers were no help, either.

Tommy said, "What a waste of time to go watch you lose to the Bears." Kenny's bad mood soured more.

Kenny wished he never played hockey. He wondered why he plays at all. It's not for him. But he knows, *it's the Conley tradition, it's what the family does.* His brothers love it and are good at. He's not. He doesn't like it. He's the loser.

Casey came over to the Conley house, just like after

most games. They all talked about the game for hours. Casey was mad they lost but not mad at Kenny. She liked Kenny and she knew what Kenny was like; he wasn't the most competitive kid.

Legacy

Kenny woke up the next morning and got ready for school. He knew the topic would be the game last night and him failing to score. *What a fun day,* he thought.

Mom was waiting in the kitchen; she hadn't said much last night so it must be her turn now.

She talked about the schedule for tonight. "Kenny, your practice is at 7. Tommy your game is in Duluth, so you need to catch the bus at 3. Ryan are you helping coach Kenny's practice tonight or going to Tommy's game?" she asked.

"I'm going to Tommy's game. Maybe I'll see someone win tonight." Ryan shot a glance at Kenny.

Mom answered, "Now Ryan, Kenny will figure this out. You weren't always the leading scorer on your teams." Kenny thought, *is that all she wants? For me to score?* He just wanted to leave.

Kenny ran out into the cold. *Another lovely January morning in Brenton. Not bad! Five below, no wind.*

Kenny hopped on the bus and joined Casey and Paul in the back. Paul got on first, so always got the back and saved it. As Kenny passed the other kids, he could hear what he expected to hear. "Nice shot, Kenny." "Someone put cement in your gloves?"

As Kenny sat down, Casey asked Paul, "Did the coach say anything else about the game last night? We saw he kept you afterwards."

Paul nodded. "Yeah, he doesn't want me taking so many chances. 'Stay in the net where you belong.' That kinda of stuff. But I scored a goal! I tied the game."

Kenny replied, "Yeah, I wouldn't have had the chance to screw up the game if you didn't give me that lead pass."

"Oh like giving you a breakaway is a bad idea?!?" Paul

threw back at him.

Casey, knowing this would go nowhere good, decided to change the subject. "Paul, you ready for the trip to the Cities for the cake-eater tournament?"

"Yeah I can't wait to go to that hotel again. Mini-sticks, marshmallows, and swimming!" Paul quipped.

"Swimming?" Casey scoffed. "You *know* Coach won't let us swim while we're at the tournament!"

"He'd better! They have the best water slides and hot tubs!" Paul said excitedly.

"You know coach! 'We're here to win'," replied Casey in her deep coach-like voice.

Kenny knew she was right. Coach Harrington liked going down to the Twin Cities and beating the city kids. He always claimed we started the tradition of winning hockey and it was our responsibility to show them we are still the best at it.

Kenny stepped off the bus and hurried inside to warm up in the school. After the first class, Mr. Wells approached Casey and Kenny in the hallway.

"Kenny," said Mr. Wells, "We have our annual school fundraiser coming up and we need items for auction. Do you think you could talk with your dad about some items he could sign for school?"

Kenny dutifully replied, "Sure Mr. Wells, what are you looking for?"

"Well we could always use his Gopher jerseys and North Star jerseys. They always bring a great price. Maybe some gloves or sticks, too."

Casey added, "Hey, Kenny's brother Ryan is on winter break and he's playing for the Gophers now. Maybe we should get him to sign some gear, too?"

Kenny glared at Casey. *Yeah. Nice. Throw more of my family my face why don't you.*

Mr. Wells was enthusiastic. "Great idea! It's just so awesome having your celebrity family right here in Brenton. Two Gopher players now, and maybe more to come. So cool." Mr. Wells trotted off down the hall.

"Casey, isn't it bad enough I have to ask my dad for autograph stuff? Now my brother, too?" said Kenny.

"Come on Kenny, everyone would love to be in your family. Mr. Wells is right you know, being from a celebrity family."

Kenny knew that other kids were jealous of him. But it was all because they liked to watch and play hockey. Kenny didn't even like hockey, so where did that leave him in the celebrity family tradition?

"Casey, would you ask my dad and brother for the

stuff so I don't have to?" Kenny asked hopefully.

"Sure, no problem," she replied, "I got it."

Kenny walked into the rink for practice with his dad. Mom and Ryan were at Tommy's game in Duluth.

Coach Harrington called over, "Hey Cody, you bring your skates? We could use you on the ice tonight!"

Kenny's dad replied, "You betcha, don't go anywhere without 'em!"

Inside the locker room the players are giddy about Kenny's dad coming out to practice.

"Dude, it's *so cool* your dad is coaching us tonight," said one player.

"Yeah, my dad said your dad was so awesome when he played for Herb Brooks and the Gophers," said another.

Kenny just nodded. He had been through this for years now at camps, clinics, and the occasional practice.

But it had been awhile since his dad was at one of Kenny's practices. He had been going more to Tommy's high school practices, and helping out down in the Cities with visits to the Gophers with Ryan.

Kenny was always torn about his dad coming to practice. On the one hand, it was great; he liked the attention. But on the other hand, he knew he was going to get pushed and picked on.

This practice was no different. His dad barked out drills, made the players drop, get up, sprint, stop, and move constantly.

"You have to practice harder than you play in the game," he would say. "You have to earn your next win now. Can't wait 'til game time to turn it on."

He said all the things his own coaches had taught him from mite hockey up to the pros. The phrases *being a winner, paying the price, developing yourself to be the best,* just kept coming out of him like a well oiled machine.

Kenny could see the parents gathered around the outside of the boards, expectantly watching every move his dad made, listening to every word, every saying he put out there. How eager they were.

While waiting in line for his turn in a drill, he could hear the parents talking about his dad...great player, really had a way with kids... *Funny,* Kenny thought, *never really felt like he connected well with me, his own son.*

After practice, the parents were still hanging around talking. He could hear them still talking about his dad.

"How many years did he play for Herbie?" asked one.

"All four years, '76 – '79," came the answer.

"What about the Olympic team then?" asked another one.

"Cody didn't make it," came the answer. "Herb cut him early, said he didn't have the drive, the heart to win."

"He responded when he was drafted in the NHL and took the North Stars to the Stanley Cup Finals in '81."

"What happened after that?" a mom asked.

"Caught his skate in a bad rut in the ice, shattered his leg in 3 places. Never skated the same after that and had to retire."

Kenny wasn't born when his dad played pro hockey. He only heard the stories late at night around the rinks. His dad never talked about the night he broke his leg or anything after that day. Just told stories from before that fateful day. Kenny knew that's why he pushed Ryan and Tommy so hard.

Cody walked over as the kids were getting ready to leave the rink. "Great practice tonight guys. I'm sure you're ready for the tournament. Go kick some cake-eater butt."

The kids were fired up now, and Coach Harrington seemed happy, too.

"Kenny," said his dad, "Mom just called. Tommy won

his game, 6-3. He had a hat trick."

Good - at least they have that to talk about now and forget about my penalty shot, Kenny sulked.

Mariucci

Kenny woke up early on Friday morning. *Kinda nice to skip school today and take a bus down to the Twin Cities*, he groggily thought. One of the side-benefits of playing hockey was how much school you get to miss.

Sometimes it's leaving early for Tommy's game. Other times they'd try and see a Gopher game when Ryan was nearby like Duluth or Bemidji.

The families all go to the ice arena parking lot to meet the bus. "Kenny," said his mom, "You remember to bring all 3 sticks?"

"Yes, mother."

"What about your toothbrush and extra socks?" she continued.

It was the same for all the players, last minute "hockey moms" checking to make sure their kids were ready for the big trip.

The players loaded their hockey bags underneath the bus and then filed onboard. Players made sure they got the back of the bus and left the front seats for the parents.

The ride was about 4 hours to the Twin Cities. As they neared the Cities, the players watched as they got off the freeway near downtown.

The bus driver turned down 4th street. Kenny thought for a moment, *this isn't right.*. This is taking us to the University of Minnesota campus.

The bus drove slowly down 4th street and through the University of Minnesota campus. Frank looked out the window and said, "Dude, look it's Mariucci."

Sure enough, the bus stopped in front of Mariucci Arena, home of the Minnesota Golden Gopher Hockey team.

The kids erupted with questions, "What's going on?

Why are we stopping here?" The players were excited!

Kenny saw his dad hop out of his truck; he had been following the bus and Kenny hadn't noticed. The bus driver opened the door and his dad climbed on.

"Okay guys, I have a surprise for you! The Gophers have a game tonight, too, and we thought it might be a good idea to have a pre-game skate together."

The players rushed off the bus, grabbed their gear, and ran into the legendary building. Inside, they saw posters of former Gopher players and teams.

"Dad, is there a poster of you?" Kenny asked in awe.

His dad led him around the corner and there it was - a plaque with his team from 1979, National Champions. Kenny felt a bit of pride knowing his family was represented in this great arena.

"Kenny, are you going to skate?" called out Casey. Kenny nodded and raced towards her.

The players hurried, suited up, and joined the Gophers on the ice. They were playing around and having fun. The Gophers moved into drills and played some games and Kenny realized the Gophers do the same things they did at practice, only faster.

At one point, Frank yelled out, "Hey, we're playing the cake-eaters tonight."

One of the Gophers blasted back, "Hey, careful! I was a cake-eater."

His buddy next to him answered back, "You're still a cake-eater."

The jeering went back and forth until the Gophers Head Coach skated out to center ice. "Hey guys, thanks for coming out. We need to prepare for our game now, but good luck, and take it to those cake-eaters. Let's bring it in and get a cheer. Prairie Dogs on 3. 1,2,3... Prairie Dogs!"

Kenny's dad yelled out to the Gopher Coach, "Thanks coach!"

Coached yelled back, "Ya, you betcha..."

The Prairie Dogs arrived at the tournament and found their locker room. The players were still buzzing from skating with the Gophers and everyone was complimenting Kenny.

"Dude, your dad is so cool!"

"Yeah, your family is awesome!"

This made Kenny feel proud and weird. It was cool skating with the Gophers, but it still just didn't give him the desire to play hockey.

The Prairie Dogs took the ice for the warm up. The players looked over at the cake-eaters wearing their beautiful shiny green and gold jerseys.

Casey turned to Kenny and said, "You know why their uniforms are green?"

Kenny shrugged his shoulders.

"Because there are made out of money," she laughed.

The Prairie Dogs were a confident team, having just played with the Gophers, and they started the game out great, controlling the play. Yet, there was no score after the first period.

During the first intermission, the coach brought the team over to the bench.

"Guys, we are not going to let these city players keep up with us! We have got to get physical and start pushing these guys around. Stop letting them get in the zone! Hit 'em! Now let's get it done!"

The players cheered and got back on the ice. Casey started on the faceoff and pushed the center man down on the ice and took the puck. She drove to the net but was pushed wide. Brian was right behind her; she dropped the puck and Brian went to take a shot. He faked and saw Kenny streaking to the goal. Brian moved around the defensemen who just bought his fake and moved the puck over to Kenny who buried the puck into an almost empty net. Prairie Dogs 1, cake-eaters 0.

Kenny skated fast over to the bench, celebrating with Brian and Casey.

Coach looked over at them. "About time guys, we need more!"

Kenny looked over at Casey and Brian with disgust. *Come on! How about some love?*

The game continued as both teams got very physical and the play started to get rough. Casey was getting pushed around and the referee was not calling the boarding and late hits. After another late hit she took her stick and slashed back at the player. Sure enough she got called for slashing.

Coach yelled out, "Start calling the late hits!"

The cake-eaters went on the power play and scored.

Casey came out of the penalty box and slammed her stick into the bench area. "Let's go!" she screamed. Casey was angry.

The second period ended and the score was 1-1. Coach Harrington was now furious that the game was tied. He knew everyone was watching the game and his team wasn't winning.

"I know these guys are bigger than you. Some think they're faster than you. Now we're here to win. So what are you going to do? Let's get some heart and get back to the basics. Win every race for the puck, win every battle on the boards. You do that, you will win."

Kenny looked at Casey. He could tell when she got intense. Her blue eyes were wide open but not looking at anything. Kenny noticed the sweat dripping from her nose, and her lower lip trembling.

Kenny looked at Paul. He was doing the goalie tradition to focus himself, hitting the pipes, hitting his leg pads, testing his arm pads.

Paul, like most goalies, was very superstitious. He always had to be first player on the ice and last one off. He'd also loved watching Patrick Roy as a kid and adopted his style of never skating over a blue line or red line, always jumping over instead. Kenny never noticed until Casey pointed it out to him. Now he found it quite funny.

Casey didn't even listen for the coach to see who was starting; she simply skated to the faceoff circle at center ice and stood there. She said something to Brian as he skated by. The puck dropped and she did not go for the puck but lifted the cake-eaters stick and slammed herself right into him and kicked the puck back to Brian who was right there to pick it up. Kenny knew the play and sprinted behind Brian, allowing Brian to be onsides.

The two of them were both entering the zone at full speed.

Casey held her guy for as long as she could without getting called leaving the middle wide open for Brian and Kenny. Brian faked a pass to Kenny. Kenny then pretended to shoot. The goalie lost track of the puck, thinking Kenny was shooting. Brian then had an easy corner to pick and score. Prairie Dogs 2 – cake-eaters 1.

Kenny watched from the bench as him team worked hard. With a minute left the cake-eaters had to pull their goalie to try and tie the game.

Paul was strong in the net, turning away the shots and making no attempt on any big clears. He stayed in the net just like coach wanted. At one point Frank took the puck away along the boards and fired it down the ice. The puck banked off the boards and into the net. Just like they had practiced a million times in the outdoor rink back home! Prairie Dogs win 3-1.

Coach Harrington walked into the locker room after the game, and invited Casey in; she always had to dress outside the locker room.

"Guys, I am really disappointed with lack of effort and not beating the cake-eaters bigger. We are here to win and you better get that through your heads now! We're going back to the hotel now; no one is to go swimming. No running around. Get back, eat and get in your rooms. We have an early game tomorrow against the Canadians."

With that he stormed out of the room. Brian yelled "Hey, someone should tell him we WON the game!" The team was pretty upset. Coach Harrington was never happy.

The team walked out of the locker room and the parents cheered out their congratulations. The parents knew the rule about swimming and that coaches felt swimming always took too much out of players to play well the next day. The parents felt bad for the kids, but no one ever stood up to the coach.

After dinner the team met in the hotel common area. It was a great hotel with a large open area for teams. Ping pong tables, arcade, pool, basketball and volleyball courts. Kenny stared at the huge water slide going into the pool.

Casey and Brian were playing ping pong, Paul and Frank were on the floor with mini-sticks. You can't go to any hotel and not bring your mini-sticks to play floor hockey. He remembered last year having a mini-stick tournament for hours until the hotel security chased them back into their rooms.

Kenny roamed over to the basketball area and started shooting around. None of the other players joined him, but a team from Arizona was there. Teams from all over the country came to Minnesota to play hockey. They came to play in the hot bed of hockey.

Kenny hopped into a basketball game with boys from Arizona. Just as the game started, some parents from his team wandered over. "Kenny I don't think coach wants you guys getting worn out."

Kenny was mad that they'd actually approach him about this. He barked back, "Coach said no swimming. This is basketball." The parents moved away.

Sure enough, here came Coach Harrington. Kenny knew he would lose this argument so he just walked away from the basketball game and walked past the Coach, who didn't even say a word. *What a waste,* Kenny thought, *coming here to this awesome hotel and not being able to do anything.*

The next morning the Prairie Dogs were playing the team from Thunder Bay, Canada. The team from Canada had a different age cut-off that allowed them to be six months older. At this age that could mean a huge difference. And it was. The Thunder Bay team had three kids already over 6 feet tall.

The game was rough and the Canadians used their size advantage well, moving the Prairie Dogs off the puck and hard into the boards. As the game went on Kenny, Brian, and Casey would slow down to avoid being blasted against the boards. As you would expect, the coach was not happy about that.

"Come on guys! We need to get the puck back! You've got to go in the corners and win those battles."

Kenny always laughed at 'corners'. He'd been around rinks all his life; it's an oval! There are no corners on the ice. But this was no time to make fun of the coach; they were losing 2-4.

As the Canadians extended their lead they started to chirp at each other. Not so much teasing the Prairie Dogs, but each other. Kenny thought the way they talked was funny, too.

"You see my shot Jimmy? That was wonky, eh?"

Kenny would just turn his head and smile. *What the heck does 'wonky' mean?* They were certainly having fun. Kenny wondered if they had been able to go swimming last night.

The coach came into the locker room after the game.

"Okay guys, we're out of the championship game

thanks to that performance. We play at noon tomorrow against the team from Arizona for third place." He paused. "Well since swimming is for losers, guess what! You can swim tonight. Lights out at ten." With that the coach stormed out of the locker room.

Kenny looked excitedly at Brian, but his team did not seem excited like he was about swimming. Kenny was thinking about going down the water slide and playing games in the water. Being tournament champions really didn't mean much to him. On the other hand, water parks were fun!

But his teammates were upset about not going to the championship and he then realized they all had to face their parents outside the locker room. *Oh yeah...we gotta get back to the hotel before we can look excited to swim.* Kenny put on his somber face.

It was a much lighter mood on Saturday night as the team swam and played mini-sticks. The players were really having a good time. Kenny thought *it's not that bad to lose if you get to have fun.* But he knew Casey did not feel this way. She was playing ping pong and talking with Kenny's dad. Kenny knew she was disappointed about not going to the championship game. He watched as her pony tail swung from side to side as she played.

He did like her, and thought she was cute, but that's not something you walk up and tell your hockey line mate.

The next day came and Casey and Brian each scored a hat trick and they won third place by a score of 9-1. Paul was even upset about giving up the one goal. But he had gotten bored and was not paying attention when they scored. Kenny felt bad for the guys he was playing basketball with Friday night. But how many ice rinks could they even have in the whole state of Arizona? Did they even have any outdoor rinks?

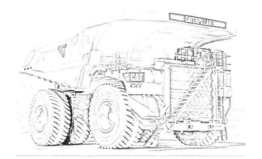

Mine

Winter came to an end and Kenny was able to get outside and do more of what he wanted. But spring gave way to summer and that meant summer hockey. Kenny's brother, Ryan, ran a summer hockey camp in town. That meant Kenny was expected to help out at the camp.

One day, as Kenny was resisting going to the rink and his mom was down in the Cities, he asked if he could go to work with his dad instead.

Cody worked at Brenton Creek Mining as a supervisor. He got the job after his injury in the NHL. The boss was a big fan of Cody's and wanted to give him a job to keep him in town so he would coach his kids in hockey.

"Can I ride on one of the big dump trucks today?" Kenny asked hopefully. He'd never paid much attention when his dad talked about work, except when it involved one of the massive dump trucks.

The trucks Kenny was referring to were not your typical dump trucks. The tires alone stood taller than his dad's truck and the dump trucks were bigger than a two story house.

"We'll see," his dad answered, "Maybe we can get inside one and let you see how it feels."

Kenny was excited to see the trucks again and thought about how fun it would be to drive one.

"Remember while we're there, no messing around. This equipment is big and can't be easily stopped. I don't want you getting hurt and missing any of your next season," his dad said.

It was always about hockey with his dad. Do this, don't do that, hockey, hockey, hockey.

As they were driving by the park outside town, Kenny noticed a couple of guys throwing a ball around. Not with a baseball glove, but sticks with nets on the end.

Kenny was fascinated and watched as they threw and caught the ball with ease. Then they shot at the hockey nets that were sitting in the outdoor rinks.

"What are those sticks?" Kenny asked with interest.

His dad answered in a bored voice, "Oh those are lacrosse sticks. I've seen 'em play in Canada. Kinda for the boys who can't skate well enough to play hockey."

There was another shot at anything that wasn't hockey. But Kenny was mesmerized. The car was past the park now, but Kenny craned his neck so he could keep watching as long as he could.

"How do you play? Do you shoot at a net? Do you get to play outside?" Kenny was too excited to even let his dad answer.

Dad interrupted, "Kenny, no one plays lacrosse in Brenton. There are no teams to play on. We're a hockey town. Just leave it alone. They must be visiting from out of town."

But Kenny was too intrigued to leave it alone.

They reached the mining office and his dad took Kenny over to the dump trucks right away. Probably figured he needed to distract Kenny away from that lacrosse stuff and get him inside his favorite dump truck.

They walked over to the largest truck on the lot. The chief foreman, Dan Nelson, hopped out of his truck to meet Cody.

"Hey Cody. Bringing the young one out for a look?"

"Yah, Kenny wants a look at our new big boy."

Dan proceeded to give Kenny a complete overview of the new company dump truck.

"Kenny, this here is the Caterpillar 797F. We call her Lena. She can carry up to 400 tons of rock. She's got a V-20 diesel engine, and stands over 50 feet tall when raised. The tires alone are over 13 feet tall, and she'll top out at over 40 miles per hour."

Kenny was definitely getting distracted now looking at the huge size of the truck.

"The tires alone cost $40,000 dollars each and there are six of them. She cost us a good five million dollars to get here."

Cody chimed in, "Okay so why is she sitting around for that price?"

Dan chided back, "We are just checking her out making sure she's ready to go. We'll get her moving, you betcha."

Dan pointed for Kenny to climb the stairs up to the cab. Kenny looked around from the perch of the driver's cab, and felt proud to be up that high. *On top of the world,* he thought.

As Kenny climbed down, he saw a large man walking towards them. He had lots of long curly black hair so you couldn't see much of his face. He was wearing a Brenton Creek Mining security uniform. He stood well over six feet tall and probably weighed over 300 pounds.

Cody called out to him, "Briggs, what's got you out during the day?"

Briggs grumbled, "Kids were up here again last night messing around. I chased them off but it's been three times this week, boss."

Cody asked, "How are they gettin' in? Hole in the fence? They take anything?"

"No, didn't take anything, just poking around in the shafts," answered Briggs.

"Good. You know who it was at all?" asked Cody.

"It's not the local kids. No blondes among them. All had black hair."

Kenny knew what he meant. Most of Brenton was Norwegian through and through. A blonde, blue-eyed group of Lutheran immigrants. People rarely moved to Brenton and even fewer moved out. Briggs had meant the Native Americans. They had an area a little west of

Brenton.

Now the local teens would dare each other at times to go into the shafts. They were all terrified of Briggs. He was a loner who used to live in the caves outside of town.

The local kids say that Briggs killed Ricky, a local kid who went into the cave. Briggs went to prison for several years. When Briggs was released, Kenny's dad hired him as a security guard.

His dad would say, "Who's gonna mess with Briggs when they all think he killed that kid? I want him on my side if anything happens around here."

Kenny heard his dad talk about the incident with other miners. He said Briggs had heard Ricky screaming for help after falling down a 15-foot shaft. The other kids had dared Ricky to go into the dark cave, and he fell out of their reach.

The kids all scattered when Briggs came to help, afraid they'd get in trouble for being in the cave. The shaft caved in on Ricky and Briggs. When the rescue team reached them, they pulled Briggs out alive with a broken shoulder. But Ricky had been crushed by the rocks. The kids were too scared to tell the truth. Instead they testified against Briggs, saying he threw Ricky down the shaft, killing him.

All Kenny knew was Briggs scared him. He was relieved that dad needed to get back to his office.

As Kenny walked away from the big truck, he heard Dan yell out to the driver, "Alright Bob! Let's go put the rock in the box!"

Kenny and his dad went back to his office and his dad went into a meeting. This gave Kenny time to think about lacrosse again. He wondered if those boys were still there and where they were from. Dad seemed pretty sure nobody in town played lacrosse and Kenny had never even seen a lacrosse stick before.

Kenny walked out of the office and told the guys, "If my dad's looking for me I'm going to the park to hang out."

Kenny walked back to the park and sure enough, the boys still throwing and catching. He watched for a minute before he approached. He figured they were about two years older than him. He noticed they both had on shorts that said Frost. He figured they must play together on the same team.

Kenny started with a simple, "Hey."

The players responded, "Hey, what's your name?"

"Kenny. Kenny Conley," he replied.

The boys stopped throwing. "We saw you at the camp earlier this week, right?"

Kenny was there, but he didn't remember these two.

"Yeah I was there," Kenny stuttered a bit.

"Is Ryan your brother?" they asked.

Kenny nodded.

"Cool, he's an awesome player. Our brothers are at his camp in town. My name's Jack, this is Scott."

"Where you guys from?" asked Kenny.

"Twin Cities," answered Scott, "Jack's from Burnsville, I'm from Prior Lake. South side of Cities."

Kenny replied, "Yeah, we went down your way this winter for the cake-eater tournament. We took third place."

Jack said, "Yeah, we saw you. My brother's team lost to Thunder Bay in the championship game.

"Must be cool having a dad who played in the NHL and a brother playing for the Gophers," commented Scott.

"I guess," shrugged Kenny, "But I don't like hockey that much."

"Oh that must go over well with the family," chuckled Jack.

Kenny answered, "Yeah, makes for fun winters. I play

of course, just don't have a choice."

"You play?" asked Scott gesturing with his lacrosse stick.

"Nah, we're not big on sports other than hockey here," answered Kenny.

"We play hockey, too, but lacrosse is something fun to do in the summer instead of hockey. You can only do so much dryland," said Jack.

Kenny could relate to that. Dryland training was all the off-ice stuff to improve your game. Stick handling with rolling pucks, Russian boxes, slide boards, roller hockey, and shooting outside for hours on end.

"Wanna try it?" offered Scott.

"Sure!" said Kenny. He grabbed the stick and it felt foreign to him. Kenny was used to sticks pointing at the ground, not in the air.

"Okay, first thing, it's the opposite of hockey," said Scott, showing Kenny how to hold the stick.

"The end hand in hockey controls the stick. In lacrosse it's the other hand. Let your bottom hand relax. Hold the lacrosse stick with your fingers, not in the palm of your hand."

Kenny listened intently as Scott walked him through holding and cradling the stick. Kenny tried to throw the ball but *plop* right to the ground.

Scott encouraged him, "Don't worry about it, just get use to the motion. Snap your wrist. Also make sure you pull with your bottom hand, don't just push."

Kenny kept trying, and started throwing and catching. He looked up a few times just to enjoy the feeling of being in the sun. He could really like this being-in-the-sun-playing-a-game thing!

Kenny asked, "What does the Frost mean?"

Jack answered, "Oh just a traveling lacrosse team we play on. There aren't a lot of teams in Minnesota, so we travel back east to play some of the good teams. We're called the Minnesota Frost."

"Back east?" asked Kenny.

"Oh yeah, lacrosse is huge back east. Maryland, Pennsylvania, New Jersey, New York. It's big-time out there. And it's now the fastest growing sport in the country, including Minnesota. They grow up playing it out there. They are way ahead of us right now."

Kenny had never even heard of lacrosse. *How come I've never heard of this?*

Kenny asked, "Where is it from? Who started it?"

Jack said, "It's actually an original sport from the Native Americans. They had several Nations who played in

North America. The French saw them playing it. They called it lacrosse. Later the Canadians picked it up and put together rules to play by."

Scott blurted out, "Yeah, it was the first official sport of Canada, before hockey. Now they call it the official summer sport of Canada."

"So why is it so big on the east coast?" ask Kenny.

"Really don't know," said Jack. "They tried to make it an Olympic sport but it never really caught on. Only three countries really play it, England, Canada, and the United States."

Kenny observed, "The ball is really hard. Doesn't it hurt when you get hit?"

Jack answered, "Oh yeah, but you wear pads and a helmet."

Kenny kept on asking questions. He was so interested to learn about the field they played on, how many players, penalties, and plays they ran.

He tried learning the new terms too: cradling, man up, and fun terms like 'yard sale'. Yard sale was when you hit the stick out of another players hand, it lands on the grass like it's laying in a front yard having a yard sale.

As the afternoon wore on he knew he'd better get

back to his dad's office. Kenny said goodbye to the Frost players and ran back.

As Kenny arrived at his dad's office he blurted out, "Dad, I went to the park and talked with those guys playing lacrosse!"

Dad answered without looking up, "Yah."

Kenny kept going, "Yah, they have brothers in Ryan's camp and they play for the Minnesota Frost. They travel back east and play the teams there. I tried it; it's pretty fun, a lot like hockey, dad!"

"Kenny, how many times do I need to tell you, you're not playing lacrosse? It's for kids who can't skate. You can skate, you're a hockey player, and we're a hockey family."

Kenny stopped listening. He tossed the ball Scott gave him in the air. Weighed the same as a puck only baby blue and round.

Kenny wondered how to get his own stick. He had never seen them in the sporting good stores in town.

"Dad, I want a lacrosse stick for helping out at Ryan's clinic. Mom said I can get something for helping out."

His dad answered, "Yah, sure, whatever."

Yes! thought Kenny.

Cave

Kenny woke up early the next morning and rode his bike to the park. He wanted to meet up with the Frost boys again and see where he could buy a stick.

But at the park he did not see the Frost boys. He sat around wondering where they might be. He decided to ride back towards town and go to the rink. As Kenny started to leave the park he looked up the hill and noticed a cave. He remembered that might be the cave where Ricky died.

Kenny was curious about what had happened between Briggs and Ricky. Kenny wanted to investigate. Kenny rode up the hill towards the cave. The cave had a small opening that had some boards with signs warning people to keep out.

The ground around the area was very dark red. Red is the color the soil gets when there is a lot of iron ore. The ore is loaded into the large dump trucks, and then put into rail cars where it's transported to Duluth on the shore of Lake Superior. From there the ore is loaded onto ships that take it from Lake Superior out via the lower Great Lakes. The ore then is taken to steel plants that melt the ore and turn the iron into steel.

As Kenny rode up the hill, he realized it was too steep to bike. He stepped off his bike, and walked up the suddenly steeper hill. As he approached the opening of the cave he could read the signs to 'KEEP OUT'.

Kenny looked to see if anyone was around. The hill had several trees around it and the cave was about half way up the hill. As he entered the cave he walked slowly, waiting for something to happen. *Aren't bats supposed to fly out if I walk in? Would there be a bear?* He made a lot of noise, kicking rocks and dirt, to let who or whatever might be in there know he was there. He listened hard, but thankfully heard nothing and saw no movement.

Kenny remembered he had a flashlight mounted to his bike. His mom had gotten it for him in case he had to ride home from the rink in the dark. He grabbed the flashlight and decided to head into the dark cave.

Kenny wasn't sure why he was so obsessed about looking in the cave, but he needed to see. Maybe he could find the shaft where Ricky fell. Kenny turned on the flashlight and started walking very slowly into the pitch-black cave. The cave turned quickly to his right and soon the front of the cave was out of sight. No daylight. It was dark. His pulse quickened but he was determined.

Kenny looked around, very scared at first. He could see the light shaking in front of him, and his hand would not stay still. Kenny's eyes started to adjust to the low light and he could see writing on the wall. Kids had been in here before. Notes written to Ricky, words to kill Briggs, and arrows pointing the way.

Kenny now felt compelled to follow the arrows. *I have to see what's there*, he thought to himself. But then he wondered, *should I go back? Have someone come with me? Casey, Paul, or Tommy?* He knew they wouldn't want to come in here without a reason. Kenny didn't have a reason, he had a mission, and he had to see the shaft where Ricky fell.

He followed the arrows and the cave started getting smaller, turning more and more, going downhill. What if his flashlight broke? That had never crossed Kenny's mind until just now. He kept going. Suddenly the arrows changed to "STOP."

The next arrow pointed down, and there in front of him was an opening in the ground. *The shaft,* Kenny thought. He got on his hands and knees and started crawling towards the hole. There were old busted wooden braces all around the shaft.

Kenny took his flashlight and peered into the hole. It went far down, and at first Kenny could not see the bottom. He dropped a couple of rocks in, to hear when they stopped. They hit pretty quickly and his eyes adjusted to see the bottom. He could see some burned-out flares where people had dropped them into the hole before.

Kenny leaned forward to see better, and lost his grip on the old wooden brace. His hand slipped and he fell. He reacted by reaching up and grabbed one of the boards and held on. Kenny was now holding on for his life. He could see above him the light from his flashlight and below the shaft was pitch black. *I'm not falling down there,* he thought, *not now.*

As Kenny struggled to pull himself up, he thought, *why was Ricky in here? Did Briggs drag him in here? Was Ricky exploring the cave and fell? Which story should I believe?* Kenny pulled his body up with his arms and pushed with his feet on the side of the shaft. As he dragged himself over the top he rolled, exhausted and gasping for air.

Kenny laid there glad to be alive. As he regained his strength to sit up, Kenny rolled over and his flashlight was pointing away from the shaft, down the cave.

The light was pointing towards a wall in the cave. As Kenny sat there to calm down, he noticed a large boulder. Near the bottom of it was a small hole in the wall of the cave. He struggled to his feet. He walked over to the hole near the boulder. He took his flashlight and shown it inside. He saw it opened into another area.

Kenny was really curious now. Maybe Briggs hid something in there. The hole was small but Kenny managed to squeeze through.

As he got to the other side he realized he was in a

large room. He looked around and saw an object at the far side. At first he thought his eyes were just messed up. But as he moved closer, sure enough; it was a large flat stone.

This stone was very dark and had symbols on it. Triangles, claws, eyes, and what appeared to be feather prints. He touched the stone. It was made of a smooth hard stone and was very cold. He thought *maybe this opens. Maybe it's a box to keep something in.* He looked around for a way to open it. But there were no handles or knobs or any way to open it.

He tried to lift the stone box but it was too heavy. There was no way he was carrying this box out of the cave.

After several minutes of trying to find a way in, he realized it was no use. He looked down and saw his flashlight was going dim. The batteries are dying. *Better get out here* he nervously thought.

As he crawled back out of the hole it was then he realized he was on the other side of the shaft and would have to cross back. Kenny threw his flashlight to the other side. He backed up and took a running leap, jumping over the shaft. As he jumped he easily cleared the shaft but jumped so far he slammed in the cave wall on the far side. BAM! Kenny was glad he hadn't fallen in, but his face felt bloody.

Kenny knew where he needed to go next. He had to tell Casey.

Kenny knocked on Casey's door. She lived in a small house near the park. Casey answered the door and saw Kenny covered in dirt and bleeding from his face.

"Nice look," she teased. "Were we playing with the dump trucks again?" Kenny didn't even realize he was covered in dirt from the cave.

"Casey, you'll never guess what I found!" said Kenny.

Casey could tell Kenny was overly excited. "Okay, come in, but don't touch anything," she said.

Kenny started, "Okay, but don't freak out, everything is fine."

Casey's mind started to race. *Why would he start by saying everything's okay?* "What happened?" asked Casey, "What did you do?"

"I went up to the cave where Ricky died."

Casey interrupted, "What? When? Today?"

Kenny looked irritated, "Yes, let me tell you."

"Who did you go with?" Casey persisted.

"I went by myself, okay? I know it was stupid, but I had to see. I became obsessed. I needed to go in there!"

said Kenny.

"Kenny, Ricky died in there! Why would you go there alone? Do you have any idea how dangerous that was?" said Casey as her voice began to get louder.

"Casey, I'm okay! You can yell at me later. Listen! I found something. I found a stone box near the shaft where Ricky fell," said Kenny. "It was big, and dark, and was really, really heavy. I couldn't lift it or I would have brought it over here."

Casey went from being upset at Kenny to being a little curious. She asked, "What kind of box? Was it like a tool box or something someone hid, or –"

"No." Kenny interrupted Casey's barrage of questions. "It was made of stone, a dark black rock of some kind. I couldn't find a lid or latch or door, or any way in. It did have some engravings like triangles, claws, and feather-like prints. It was really dark and black and I wouldn't have found it if I didn't almost fall when I was looking down into the shaft."

"When you what?" scolded Casey. "What happened? Did you get hurt? What were you thinking?"

"Okay mom, I know," answered Kenny sarcastically.

Casey decided to change tactics.

She said softly, "Kenny, Ricky is dead because he fell

in there, and he wasn't even alone.

Kenny remembered Ricky was with a group of friends, who ran off when Briggs came to help; or finish him off. Kenny didn't really know which.

"What do you think it is?" Casey continued as she calmed down.

"Well it's about four feet long and about two feet wide and two feet high. It looks really old and was very smooth in places."

Casey thought about it and wondered aloud, "Do you think it could be a coffin? Like for a kid?"

Kenny jumped back a bit. "A coffin? That's really creepy. Why would you think that?"

She hesitated, then said, "I think we should go back. I need to see what it is you're talking about."

Kenny asked mockingly, "I thought you said it was too dangerous to go in there?"

Casey snapped back at him, "We're not going alone. We're going in together to investigate, and if something happens to one of us the other one can go for help."

Kenny added, "I'll grab my brother's cell phone, too. Tomorrow is Sunday. He won't miss it before noon. We can go early, first thing in the morning."

Kenny rode his bike home in the dark, his mind thinking about the stone box. *What could be in the box? Would they find a body inside? Could it be a coffin, like Casey suggested?* Once home, he ran inside and straight to the family computer in the living room.

Kenny searched for, "black stone box", and looked for clues online. Kenny thought, *if anyone knows about it, it will be on the internet, right?* Searches come back for a lot of things. Kenny clicked a hundred sites but nothing that looked even close. He called up his Facebook page and saw Casey online. She had also been searching and couldn't find anything.

As Kenny chatted online with Casey, his parents told him it was bedtime, and to get off the computer. He begged for 5 more minutes. He wanted more time to talk about the stone box with Casey. But his parents insisted. He grudgingly logged off and stomped to his room.

Kenny laid awake all night, wondering what it was he had found. At 7am he jumped out of bed, grabbed his brother's cell phone, and raced his bike to Casey's. She was already waiting outside on her bike.

They rode past the park and up the hill. Kenny got off his bike as before and walked it up the hill. Casey followed his lead. While they walked, Casey told him what she had brought along. She was prepared! And he was impressed. She had brought multiple flashlights, a hammer, screwdriver, rope, an air horn from her dad's boat, and hockey tape. *You can always find a use for hockey tape,* Kenny thought.

At the entrance to the cave, Casey paused and turned to Kenny. "Whatever happens, we stay together."

Kenny nodded, and pointed to the boards on the ground. "We can lay these over the shaft, so we can walk across."

They took a deep breath, looked at each other, then entered the cave. Kenny pointed out the arrows on the wall. Casey stopped to read a few items. 'RIP Ricky', 'We love you Ricky', 'Briggs must die!'

Kenny pointed to the arrow, "This way."

They continued through the cave as it narrowed, until they reached the arrow that pointed down. Kenny knelt down and slid the boards across to make a bridge over the shaft. They carefully walked across the boards and safely reached the other side.

Casey squinted at an opening near the boulder. "You fit through *this* hole?" she asked skeptically.

Kenny smiled. "You never stop, do you?" Kenny

crawled in first to prove that yes...he had!

And there it was, right in front of them. Casey grabbed the other flashlights out of her bag and turned them all on. It was just like Kenny had described, only now they could see the engravings better.

Kenny looked and saw the eyes for the first time, eyes carved into the stone, claws, pointed ears. And the box was very cold.

Casey stared at it, "Kenny, do you think they look like owls?"

Kenny moved closer, and Casey was right. The claws, the eyes, the pointed ears – it did look like owls. "Yeah, they do look like owls," he said. "What do you think that means?"

Casey was thinking back to all the things she saw on-line. "This is nothing like anything I saw on the web last night," she said while looking at Kenny.

Kenny leaned back on his heels. "So, how do you think it opens?"

Casey looked back at the stone box. "You think it opens? What if it's just a stone somebody carved on?"

Kenny was starting to get agitated. "It must open. There has to be something inside. Why would they hide it in a room behind a large boulder if it didn't have something valuable in it?"

Casey thought that made sense. She could also see that Kenny had become obsessed with the stone box.

Kenny was grabbing and touching everything he could find. "Casey, let's lift it up. Maybe it's just a cover over something."

They each stood at an end of the box, grabbed on and lifted. "Whoa!" Casey yelled out. They were not going to be able to begin to budge the box.

"It's way too heavy," Kenny said in frustration.

They sat down and tried to think. *Was this a box or just a stone with carvings on it? Was Casey right? Was it just a rock? If so, was there a message? A treasure map perhaps?*

As morning wore on Casey and Kenny sat there thinking. Trying to coming up with ideas. Then trying their ideas. But, nothing was working. Both were sure it had to mean or be something.

6

Stick in the Stone

As Casey and Kenny sat in the cave looking at the stone box, Kenny decided to inspect it closer. He pulled out a screwdriver from Casey's bag.

"Maybe I need to move something. You know, like in those Indiana Jones movies. Maybe there's a secret combination."

Casey rolled her eyes, "Yep, just like in the movies."

Even though Casey thought Kenny's ideas were far-fetched, she wasn't sure what to do, either. *The stone box was here just like Kenny described,* she thought. *It may be just a big rock with nothing inside. It's too big to move, so what else can we do?*

She didn't discourage Kenny, but it was becoming clear to her there was nothing more they could do alone.

While Casey thought about their options, Kenny probed around the claws, eyes, and all parts of the stone with the screwdriver. Kenny was focused, remembering everything he tried, every combination. *There just had to be a way in,* he kept thinking, *there has to be something inside.*

Kenny started thinking aloud, "What are owls known for? They can turn their heads all the way around," he answered himself.

Casey corrected him. "No, they can't go all the way around Kenny. They actually can only go about –"

But before she could finish, Kenny grabbed a second screwdriver. "Look! There are only two eyes on the whole stone. What if I take the screwdrivers and put them in both eyes at once, and try and turn them?"

Casey knew he wasn't listening to her. He was in la la land, obsessing. *Why didn't he work this hard at hockey?* Just as she was about to ask to leave the cave, they both heard it. CLICK.

"What was that?" Casey asked, starting to stand up.

"The eyes moved!" gasped Kenny. "Look! There is an opening!" Kenny pointed just below the eyes.

Sure enough, Casey saw a small opening. They grabbed a flash light and looked inside. As they peered in, they could only see something that looked like a bone.

"EEWWWW! It is a coffin! Don't touch it!" said Casey.

"You said it was a rock," he said distractedly.

Kenny stared inside. "What should we do?"

"We should tell someone!" insisted Casey.

Kenny thought for a moment. As he looked he saw the bone was really twisted, not one piece, but molded pieces together.

"Casey, I don't think it's a bone. It's too twisted and it's more gray than white," Kenny speculated. He went on, "Maybe it's like a lever or something to open it."

Casey answered, "Don't you even think of putting your hand in there."

He didn't know what was inside. It could be trap. If he reached in there, he could lose his hand. Or be bitten by something. Or become a hostage. Kenny was nervous.

"Casey, there is no way we can carry this thing out. But I gotta know what's in it. I'm not leaving until we figure this out," insisted Kenny.

"Be reasonable. Think about it. We can go get Paul, Frank, or your brothers and they can help us get it out of the cave. We can figure it all out together," Casey pleaded.

Kenny knew Casey was right, but he couldn't wait. Something was driving his obsession with this stone box. Kenny sat back and stared, thinking, *Why am I doing this? What's the worst that can happen? I've got a cell phone. Yeah, it won't work down here, but Casey can run to the front of the cave and use it.*

As Kenny sat there, Casey got up and started packing things up. He could tell she was determined to leave. He knew what he needed to do to keep her from just leaving. As she turned towards him again, he impulsively stuck his right hand inside the box.

"NO!" screamed Casey.

Kenny had put his hand in, but did not grab the bone-like object inside. He paused, not only to think about his next move, but to also see if anything would simply happen, on its own. *I'm doing this, I'm doing this...* He closed his eyes and grabbed the bone.

The bone was ice cold, but not for long. Kenny felt it becoming warmer. Casey watched, both horrified and hopeful. So far, Kenny looked okay.

"It's getting warmer. I can feel it."

Kenny stopped talking and Casey could see Kenny's face tighten up.

He then yelled, "IT'S HOT!"

Casey could see a grey light glowing inside the box.

Kenny was screaming in pain, "IT'S BURNING ME!"

Casey was scared now, shaking and not sure what to do. Kenny was in pain. Should she stay with him? Should she run for help?

She yelled back, "LET GO! Let go of the bone!"

But Kenny couldn't let go. The bone was burning him and he couldn't move his hand. His heart was pounding and he couldn't really think.

The light inside was getting brighter, and began to fill the entire room.

Casey was freaking out. *What was happening? How was this box holding on to Kenny? Was it a trap?*

Kenny was in pain. He couldn't think. He tried to lift the bone, but it was too heavy. He and the bone were stuck together.

Kenny felt the heat go up his arm, and into his body. But soon he couldn't feel anything at all. He passed out.

Casey knelt down and grabbed his shoulders, shaking

him.

"Kenny! Wake up!" she pleaded.

Kenny slumped down, his hand still in the box. The light was still bright. Casey started to cry, yelling, "STOP IT! STOP IT!"

It seemed like forever, but after only a minute from the time he grabbed the bone, the light started to go dim. The cave grew dark again, lit only by their flashlights. It felt colder in the dark, too. Kenny's hand slipped out of the box and went limp by his side.

"Thank god it's over," Casey mumbled out loud.

She grabbed Kenny and held him. She tapped his face with her hand. "Kenny, Kenny," she repeated. She could feel his heart pounding; he was alive, but not awake.

Time passed and Casey grabbed the cell phone. No signal. Yeah, a cave full of iron ore. No chance of a signal in here.

Casey got up, determined to make her way to the front of the cave. *Who do I call? What do I tell them? This was so dumb. Why was Kenny so obsessed with finding out what was in that stupid box?*

As she started to crawl out of the room, she heard Kenny moan.

"KENNY," she yelled as she crawled back towards him.

Kenny coughed. "What happened?"

Casey glared back at him. She was angry. "You put your hand in the box. You said it was burning you! You were screaming!"

Kenny looked down at his hand. It looked normal. He moved it. "My hand is fine," he said, surprised. He didn't remember any of it.

Just then the box made a hissing sound. A latch popped and the lid opened up.

Kenny stared wide-eyed at the stone box. Casey leaned over, and together they looked inside. The lid was about two inches thick and solid black stone. It took a moment for their eyes to adjust. Slowly the bone-shape image emerged from the darkness.

The bone was about 3 feet long, twisted and grey. It looked rough and ragged, like a twisted bone. At one end the bone ended in a hook, but the other end was much more interesting. It had the head of an owl, with pointed ears, large eyes, and beak that formed an opening. The area opened about four inches across and twelve inches high. There were feathers dangling from various spots on the bone.

Kenny was in shock. He knew there was something

special inside. And he wasn't afraid of it any more. He reached for it.

"Remember, it burned you before!" cautioned Casey.

Kenny looked at his hand. "I don't see any burns."

Casey was not going to let Kenny touch it again. "Kenny, the whole place lit up and you were knocked out. I am not letting you touch it."

"Okay, *you* touch it," he said.

"I'm not touching anything!" said Casey.

Kenny pulled back. "Okay, it's settled then. I'm touching it." Kenny quickly reached and grabbed the stick before Casey could stop him. This time, the stick did not burn or knock him out. Instead, it just started to glow a silver color.

Kenny just stared at the stick. He ran his fingers from the owl head down to the end. While it looked twisted and ragged, the bone was smooth as silk. He could move his hand along it without feeling any rough spots. He was fascinated.

Casey, however, was ready to go. She'd had enough for one morning.

"Kenny, we gotta go," she said while standing up. "I don't know what happened, but you got your box open and now we need to leave before something else bad happens." She was becoming annoyed and angry.

"Bad? This is awesome! What do *you* think it is?" ask Kenny.

Casey grabbed his hand. "We gotta go! I need to get out of here!" she said, looking him directly in the eyes. She made her point. Kenny knew she meant it when her eyes were intense. He agreed to leave the cave, but he was bringing the stick with him. Casey rolled her eyes, but didn't try to stop him.

Kenny and Casey rode back to her house.

"What should we do with it?" she asked.

"We gotta hide it for now," he answered. "We gotta figure out what this stick is. No one is going believe us."

For the second straight night, Kenny and Casey did not get much sleep. The next day, Kenny couldn't help but tell Paul, Brian, and Frank what he and Casey had found.

Of course, they didn't believe him.

"Come on, Kenny," said Paul. "You really want us to believe you found some boney stick right next to where Ricky fell in the shaft. And nobody else saw this stick after everyone went in there to investigate. The police, the parents, Briggs. They never found this thing, but you did? Where is the stick?"

"Yeah," said Brian, "Where's the stick?"

Kenny knew better, but answered their challenge. He wanted them to believe him.

"Okay, I'll show it to you, but I have to help Ryan at his summer clinic today. I'll bring it to the park right after the clinic. You'll see," Kenny said defiantly.

7

Guardians of the Game

Kenny pulled the stick from the back of his closet. He looked at it closely. The stick was clearly made of bones, twisted bones, woven together to create a long handle about three feet long. Although the bones appeared twisted, the handle felt smoother than anything Kenny had felt before.

The bottom of the stick was a knob that hooked in one direction to secure the hand. Kenny grabbed it tight and made a throwing motion, hard, knowing his hand would never slip off the bottom of this stick.

The top of the stick had the face of a large grey owl. The owl's mouth was wide open, beyond anything that would be a normal look. The head was covered in feathers, with pointed ears on top. It was very scary looking. Inside the mouth of the owl were straps of leather, feather cores, and a mixture of items interlaced creating a pocket area.

Kenny grabbed the baby blue lacrosse ball he had received from one of the Frost players. It fit perfectly, and as Kenny cradled the stick it felt good. *This feels right. Was it an ancient lacrosse stick?*

Kenny hopped on his bike and rode over to the park. As he approached he could see Brian, Paul, and Fred waiting for him.

As he rode up he could hear his friends laughing and yelling out, "Check out the owl Kenny hit with his bike."

Kenny got off his bike and handed the stick to Frank.

"Where did you get this?" asked Frank.

"I told you guys! Casey and I found it in the cave," replied Kenny.

"There is no way this was just sitting in some cave", said Brain. "This looks like new, like someone just made this.

Paul was looking more closely and then said, "But, it also looks very old."

"What it's made of?" asked Frank.

"Looks like bone to me," said Paul.

"Kenny, what is it?" asked Paul.

Kenny answered, "I think it's an ancient lacrosse stick."

Everyone laughed. "Dude, you just learned about lacrosse last week. Now you're some expert on what an ancient lacrosse stick is?" said Frank incredulously.

"Look at it," insisted Kenny, "It has a pocket inside the owl's mouth that is a perfect opening for catching and throwing a lacrosse ball."

"Kenny, we heard how well you did at catching and throwing lacrosse balls," said Brian. "You're terrible."

Kenny grabbed the stick away from Brian and said very low, "Not now."

When Kenny grabbed the stick back, everyone noticed how the stick started to glow a strange silver color. The entire stick began to glow.

Casey watched as Kenny's eyes glossed over. She began to see just how much Kenny had grown attached to it.

Kenny dropped the baby blue lacrosse ball into the pocket and started walking towards the outdoor rink with the hockey nets still there from the winter season. Kenny stopped about half way into the rink area and turned back to his friends.

"Watch how I throw now!"

Kenny pulled his arms back and took a large step forward. He ripped a shot straight at the hockey net. You could hear the ball ping off the crossbar, sending it over fifty feet in the air. Kenny ran over and caught the ball, and shot again, this time on the run, pegging the upper left corner of the net.

Casey watched as Kenny walked back over after taking a few more shots.

"Let me try," she begged, "It's my turn."

Casey grabbed the stick from his hands and ran out to the middle of the rink. While standing there, she noticed that the stick was not glowing anymore. *Why is it different for me?* she thought. Casey stepped and threw. The ball dropped almost straight to the ground.

The group all laughed, except for Kenny.

"Nice rip, Casey. Good thing you play hockey, girl," teased Brian.

Casey tried again but the ball just dribbled out of the stick. Again and again. Kenny finally walked over, realizing she was getting mad. He offered to help, but Casey wanted none of it. She dropped the stick on the ground and stormed away.

Kenny walked back over to his friends. Just then, an old man approached the teenagers. He was older, with straggly old gray hair. He was dressed poorly, but had an earnest look about him.

"Boy," the old man called out. "Where did you learn to shoot like that?"

Kenny was slow to respond, and decided not to answer the old man at first.

Then Kenny carefully said, "Like what? How long have you been watching?"

The old man walked slowly around the boys and looked down at the stick by Kenny's side.

"Where did you get that stick?" he asked.

"It's mine," answered Kenny.

The old man looked very curiously at the stick.

"May I see it?" the old man asked.

Kenny looked around and thought, *Okay four teenage boys versus this old man. He wasn't going to get far if he tried to run. Plus, maybe he knows something.*

"Sure," answered Kenny. "You ever see one like it before?"

"Only in legends have I heard of a stick like this. I did not think the stories were real," the old man said with a sense of awe.

"What legends?" asked Kenny.

The old man paused, looking over the stick, sliding his hand slowly over the shaft. The old man carefully inspected the stick then and looked at Kenny.

He explained, "The stories are from the First Nation, Native Americans you call them. The ones who ruled this land before us. They had warriors who played this game."

Kenny blankly looked at his friends.

The old man handed the stick back to Kenny. "I do not know the legends that well, only that there were 'Guardians of the game' who taught the warriors. They had the special sticks and ruled the game."

Kenny was now very excited to learn about the guardians. "What else do you know?"

"They had special sticks, sticks made of animals," the old man said.

"What else?" eagerly asked Kenny.

"I don't know much else," said the old man.

Kenny could tell he knew something but was not sharing. "Are you scared to tell us? You know something."

The old man replied, "You need to see the Storyteller from the Nation. He knows all the stories, he can tell you all about the stick and the guardians."

Kenny looked at his friends; they were awful quiet for hearing all this stuff. *Was he the only one wanting to learn more?*

"Where can we find the Storyteller?" Kenny asked.

The old man answered, "He lives with the Nation. They say he oversees the casino on tribal land. Start at the casino; they will know where to find him. He can tell you everything. He is the keeper of the stories."

Kenny looked around and noticed that Casey had left the park. *She missed the best part,* he thought. But he also remembered she was very upset because the stick did not work for her.

Kenny walked towards his bike, then turned back towards his friends.

"You guys see which way Casey went?"

They all looked around and shrugged their shoulders.

Kenny rode over to Casey's house and knocked on the door. Casey answered the door. Seeing Kenny, she turned around and walked back into her house, leaving the door open without any real acknowledgement of him being there.

Kenny followed her into the house and started to say "Casey —"

She cut him off, "It's not fair! Why doesn't the stick work for me? You get all the luck! Great hockey dad, hockey mom, hockey brothers, hockey family."

Kenny was getting angry now. "Casey, I HATE HOCKEY! Haven't you figured that out? I know you love it. I don't tell you what to like. But don't tell me how great I have it growing up in a rink with smelly locker rooms, being cold all the time, and everyone telling you how lucky you are."

Kenny walked closer to Casey. "Look, I like that you love hockey and hanging out with my family. It's fun to watch you play, and it's fun to be your teammate and watch you score and hit the guys down. I just want to do something else with my life. I want to find something that's special for me."

"And you think this stick is it, don't you!" accused Casey.

"I'm not sure," answered Kenny, "But after you left, a man walked over and told us he heard about a stick like this. It was from the Native Americans, First Nation people he called them. They have a legend about guardians of the game and sticks made out of animals."

"What else did he say?" asked Casey, trying not to sound too interested. She was still mad.

"He said there was a Storyteller who knew more, and told me to go listen to the story from him," replied Kenny.

"I want to go see him, but I don't want to go alone." Kenny paused. "I'd like you to go with me. I need a friend who believes me."

Casey looked at Kenny, paused, then said, "Count me in. I wouldn't miss this story for the world. So where are we going?"

Kenny was smiling because Casey was interested, but then realized he hadn't thought to ask which casino.

"Well," he said rather sheepishly, "I assume it's Red Hawk. It's the closest. Let's start there. I'll ask my brother for a ride."

Kenny raced home. He found his brother in his room. "Tommy, hey, can you give Casey and me a ride to the casino tomorrow? We need to see this guy to find out more about this stick we found and –"

Tommy chuckled. "Wow, dude, slow down! Check out that wicked stick you got."

"Yeah, that's what I'm trying to tell you," said Kenny.

"That is a sweet stick! Let me see that!" said Tommy, reaching for the stick.

Kenny shoved the stick in his face.

"Scary dude, is that a real owl?" said Tommy.

Kenny was getting annoyed. "Okay, Tommy, focus," Kenny started to speak really slowly, "Can... you... take us to the c-a-s-i-n-o tomorrow?"

"Chill, little dude! They won't let you in. You're too young," said Tommy.

Kenny snapped back, "We're not going to gamble, we're going to see a guy who is going to tell us about the stick! Where it came from, who made it and stuff!"

"Alright, check it, Amy and I are going to a concert there tomorrow. I can drop you off," said Tommy.

"Cool," replied Kenny.

Tommy called out as Kenny was leaving the room, "Mom and dad know where you're going, right?"

Kenny answered, smiling, "Yah, you betcha."

Tommy thought *oh yeah this is going to be fun to explain later.*

Red Hawk Casino

Kenny woke up early and decided to try out his stick in the backyard. He was catching and throwing just like yesterday. It was truly something special, and he spent hours practicing with it.

Casey walked into the backyard; he was surprised how late it had become.

"Casey," laughed Kenny, "You ready to go gambling?"

Tommy was packing the car for the trip and called for Kenny to help get ready. Tommy wanted the car clean for Amy, his girlfriend for the last two months. They packed the car, picked up Amy, and were on their way to the casino.

As they drove, Kenny couldn't shut up about the stick and how special it was.

"You know," said Kenny, "This stick was probably made by a special chief for his son. It might be a –"

Tommy interrupted, "Come on Kenny, enough about the stick. So what, you found some old stick in a cave."

"Its not just some old stick, Tommy," argued Kenny. "It has a special meaning. It's an ancient lacrosse stick."

"Kenny, why does it even matter?" Tommy asked. "We're a hockey family anyways. Why should it matter? It's not like dad's gonna let you play lacrosse."

Casey knew Tommy had hit a nerve. She glared a *'don't start'* look at Kenny.

Then she leaned over to remind him, "He's giving you a ride."

As they neared the casino, Kenny could feel his heart beating faster. *We're close*, he thought. Kenny had not thought about anything else but getting there. *Okay you're here, now what?* Kenny starting having doubts creep in. *What if we can't get in? What if the Storyteller is not there, or won't see us?*

Tommy pulled up in front of the casino and let Casey and Kenny out.

Tommy gave Kenny instructions. "I'll come back and pick you up here after the concert. Don't make me track you down. Be right here. I mean it!"

Kenny gave a sarcastic, "Yah, you betcha," back at Tommy.

Kenny and Casey walked toward the front entrance.

Casey looked at the entrance and turned to Kenny, "How are we supposed to get in? We're not old enough to actually go into the casino."

Kenny looked at her. "I know. We a need a plan."

"Kenny, you don't have a plan?" Casey was getting annoyed again.

Two very large casino security guards were waiting for them at the entrance.

"You're too young to come in here, my friends," said the largest one.

Kenny was suddenly a bit nervous and scared. But he remembered why he was there. He wanted to hear the stories. No one was going to stand in his way.

Kenny spoke boldly, "We're here to see the Storyteller." Kenny held up his stick towards the security guys, "He is expecting us."

One of the security guards looked closely at the stick.

He then reached for the stick but Kenny pulled it

back.

Kenny insisted, "This stick is a special stick, please do not touch."

The security guard, his badge sporting the name 'Little Joe,' looked at Kenny. "We will need to announce you are here and show the Storyteller your stick. We need you to give us the stick."

Kenny went cold. *Do I really need to let these guys have the stick? Would they ever give it back? How else can we get in? There must be a Storyteller if they are going to announce us.* Kenny's mind was frozen from all the thoughts in his head. *What if I lose the stick?*

Little Joe noticed Kenny's hesitation.

Glaring at Kenny, he said, "I wonder if this stick is even real? Maybe you kids just put feathers on some stick and are trying to trick us into seeing the Storyteller?"

Kenny reacted, "It's real!" he paused, then repeated, softer, "It's real."

Kenny reached out and handed the stick to Little Joe. "Please tell the Storyteller we are waiting."

Kenny was remembering his dad's advice to act strong, and act like you know what you're doing, especially when you're scared or nervous. People will still follow you because you're confident. Be a leader.

Little Joe grabbed the stick, turned and walked inside.

Casey pulled Kenny back a few steps then whispered so the other guard could not hear. "What are you doing? You gave up your stick? What if he doesn't let you in and you lose it?" Casey knew Kenny didn't have a plan, but geez!

Kenny nodded, "I know, but I gotta risk it, I have to know, we must see the Storyteller." Kenny was keeping his eyes on Little Joe.

The security guard walked through the casino floor carrying the stick. He walked to a small, unmarked white elevator. He stepped inside and took a slow ride up. He arrived on the top floor and stepped out of the elevator. A small group of tribal leaders were assembled in the hall.

"Little Joe," asked one of the leaders, "Why are you up here?"

The security guard paused, knowing this is not his place. But he also knew of the stories of the sticks, and knew this was important and the stick looked amazing.

"A boy has brought this to me and asked to see the Storyteller."

One of the tribal leaders admonished him, "Little Joe,

you do not need to bother the Storyteller with such things. Leave him be and send the boy –"

Just then a large white door opened at the end of the hall, and a small, very elderly man walked into the hallway.

"Let me see the stick," said the elderly man, walking slowly but determinedly towards Little Joe.

Little Joe quickly moved towards the elderly man, and placed the owl stick into his hands.

The elderly man's eyes widened as he inspected the stick. He let out a small, raspy gasp. "Little Joe, you said a boy brought this to you?"

Little Joe nodded.

"Please bring him up."

The tribal leaders started whispering in the background, but Little Joe couldn't hear what they were saying. *There must be something very special about this stick if the Storyteller wants to see the boy,* Little Joe thought.

Outside, Kenny was waiting nervously. *Why is this taking so long? What's he doing?*

Kenny nervously asked Casey, "What if he doesn't come back?"

Casey knew this was why Kenny needed someone

with him. "Kenny, it's going to be alright," she assured him.

They paced around in front of the casino, waiting for the guard to return. The door finally opened and sure enough, Little Joe emerged. But to Kenny's immediate displeasure, he saw that the stick was not with him. Kenny was scared now. *Did he steal the stick?*

Kenny walked boldly towards the security guards. Little Joe could see Kenny was upset and before Kenny could say anything he said, "Follow me, the Storyteller will see you now."

Casey's jaw dropped. She was not expecting there to be a real Storyteller, or that Kenny would actually get to meet him. Little Joe turned and they followed him inside, then into the white elevator. When they got off the elevator, Casey and Kenny looked around and saw a large white door at the end of the hallway.

They were all the way up at the top of the casino. There were windows on both sides of the hallway, allowing them to look down at the whole casino. The view was amazing!

Little Joe escorted them to the door. He knocked and turned, walking away from them. Little Joe had taken a liking to Kenny and Casey.

Kenny called back to him, "Little Joe, thank you for your help."

Little Joe smiled, "The White Crane has many stories. Give him the respect he deserves and he may share them with you."

Kenny's heart jumped a bit. This must be the right person he needed to see, to listen to, and to get the story on the stick!

The large white door opened, and Kenny and Casey saw a small, elderly gentlemen standing before them dressed all in white.

"Come in, come in. I am White Crane. Many call me the Storyteller. What are your names?"

Kenny and Casey walked in and immediately realized they must remove their shoes. The room was completely white. White carpets, white furniture, white walls, white lamps, and white trim on everything. The room was almost blinding to enter.

They stared around the room, slowly moving their eyes from item to item. A white buffalo head, elk, deer, birds, and so many other items in the room. They slowly returned their gaze to the old man, who was patiently waiting for them to finish their review of the room.

"Your names," he repeated kindly. "I am White Crane."

"I am Kenny, Kenny Conley. This is my friend Casey."

Kenny saw his stick. It was sitting on the white desk. White Crane moved towards the desk. He reached and picked up the stick.

"This is an amazing stick you brought here. How did you come to posses it?"

Kenny was excited to tell his story, but also felt he should be careful and not say too much yet.

"I found it," Kenny said, truthfully but cautiously.

White Crane did not want to be toyed with and be required to ask a bunch of questions, but decided to play along for the moment.

"Where did you find it?" asked White Crane.

"In a cave," answered Kenny.

"Nearby?" asked White Crane.

"Near our park in Brenton," answered Kenny.

"Did you just find it lying on the ground?"

"No, it was locked in a stone box," said Kenny.

White Crane became more direct. "Okay, please tell me how you found this stick and why I should believe this is real?"

Kenny was feeling nervous. *Why did White Crane suddenly change his tone? Why would he not believe the stick was real? Couldn't he tell?* Kenny knew he had to be completely truthful if he wanted him to tell him about the stick.

So he started to tell his story. "Casey and I went into a cave near our park where a kid, Ricky, had died awhile back. I was exploring and found a small room. Inside the room was a stone box. The box had engravings that looked like owls. We finally figured out a way to reach inside and touch the stick."

Kenny stopped and looked at White Crane, to see if he should go on.

White Crane spoke next, "Did you feel anything when you first touched the stick?"

Kenny answered, "I don't remember but Casey told me it was painful, hot, and then it stopped."

White Crane walked around the room and started to speak. "Many people who know the legend come in here and claim they have found the stick of a guardian." White Crane paused, inspecting the stick again. He then handed it to Kenny. "I want to see you hold the stick."

Kenny took the stick from White Crane and gently held it out from his body. It started to glow a silver color, just as before.

White Crane saw the glow, but showed no reaction.

Kenny waited anxiously for White Crane's next words.

With great reverence, White Crane said, "The stick is real."

9

Legend

Kenny stood there for a moment, speechless. He had to let what he'd just heard sink in. The stick was real. He knew it. *Wait,* he thought, *a real what* ?

White Crane asked, "Let me hold the stick."

Kenny handed it back to him, and the stick lost its glow as he let go.

White Crane spoke confidently, "The stick has bonded to you. You and the stick are one. It will obey only your touch."

Kenny was beaming with excitement, but still did not understand, and needed to ask more questions.

"What is it? You said it was real. A real what?"

"You do not know the legend then?" asked White Crane. "Many people have come here trying to convince me they have found the stick of a guardian from the legend. Many people try and trick me into believing they are the new guardians of the game."

Kenny remembered what Little Joe had said: *show him respect and you may hear the stories.*

Kenny bowed his head, "I am afraid we are not familiar with your stories about the stick or the guardians. It would give us great honor to hear the story."

"Not so fast," said White Crane with a tinge of suspicion back in his voice. "If you do not know the story, how did you know to come here?"

Kenny answered quickly, to show White Crane he wasn't trying to trick him. "We met someone in the park back in town who mentioned you and told us to come here to meet you. He saw us with the stick and came to look at it."

"Did the man tell you his name?" asked White Crane.

"No," answered Kenny, "But he was older."

White Crane began to like Kenny; he had shown respect and answered his questions honestly. White Crane paused to watch Kenny's reactions.

Kenny waited as patiently as he could. The silence was driving him nuts. He kept thinking *is he going to tell me?*

White Crane finally started, but with a question. "Do you play any sports?"

Kenny answered, "Yes, Casey and I both play hockey for the Brenton Prairie Dogs."

"Have you ever seen the game your Nation calls lacrosse?" asked White Crane.

Kenny felt his face flush with excitement. He'd never heard of lacrosse until last week, and here he was, talking with a tribal Storyteller. But now he'd have to admit he really didn't know anything about lacrosse.

"Not really," he said sheepishly. "We just started learning about it last week, from some kids up from the Cities."

White Crane gestured to Kenny and Casey to sit down. White Crane waited for them to sit, then began. "Our story starts in the beginning, with the game you call lacrosse. We call it the 'Creator's Game.' The Creator put us here on this great land with the sun, and the moon. He gave us the animals to live with and teach us.

He created twelve great Nations on this land and we grew and lived in peace."

He continued, "Each Nation was given an animal that represented them. Each animal had many strong qualities from which they could base their lives and live in harmony. Nations such as the bear, the wolf, the eagle, the owl, the bison, the hawk, and others. The Nations embraced the creator, their animals, and shared the land."

"As time passed the twelve Nations grew to fight for control over certain more desirable lands. Some Nations were jealous of the other Nations. Nations allowed pride to make them want to control others, for their way of living was better".

"The Creator saw conflicts among the Nations beginning. Instead of war, the Creator gave the Nations a game. The Creator's Game. A game that helped settle their conflicts and allowed them to not only live in peace but also share in friendly competition. The Creator gave instructions that each Nation would assemble one team each fall season before the harvest."

"All Nations would come to give thanks for the harvest and compete in the games against all Nations, and a winner would be selected."

"Nations would also be allowed to use the games as a challenge. If a Nation had an argument over land or other disagreement, they could challenge the other Nation to a game. The winner of the game would then be allowed to settle the dispute on their terms."

"Now the Creator was wise and knew Nations may try to cheat, or create unfair advantages. The Creator then drew from the earth twelve sticks that each had powers beyond that of any man-made stick. Each stick was carved to resemble the bones, feathers, fur, and skulls of the Nation's animal. Each Nation was given this one stick, and one warrior would be permitted to be the 'Guardian' of the stick."

"This warrior would be able to control the competition. The stick then would be handed down from generation to generation. The warriors would be called 'Flamethrowers' or 'Guardians of the game.' The Flamethrowers would teach the game to their Nation, train them for each game, coach them, and keep the rules for each game enforced."

White Crane paused, tired from his story. Kenny and Casey turned to each other in disbelief. *Was this real or just some story,* thought Casey? She could see Kenny was in complete awe of the Storyteller.

Kenny urged him on, "Is there more to the story?"

White Crane smiled and continued, "As you see for yourself, the stick glows for the warrior who possesses the stick. By that I mean the warrior who has bonded with the stick. The stick has only one owner at a time. No one else can use the power of the stick. The handing down of the stick was a great ceremony in each Nation. When a Flamethrower died, often it was a son who received the stick. The elders in the Nation would fast for days, looking for guidance on who would be the next Flamethrower to guide their Nation."

"It was an honor above that of a chief, or any other position within the Nation. He was the spiritual leader of the warriors, trainer to those who would honor the Creator's Game. He was the teacher of honor, respect, and physical performance."

Kenny was trying to take it all in. This was a lot more story than he had expected. He knew that the Storyteller had finished. He wanted to ask some questions, but he was afraid of offending White Crane.

Cautiously, he asked, "What happened to the Flamethrowers? Why was this owl stick buried?"

Kenny could see White Crane was uncomfortable with his questions. White Crane wandered the room again, this time pacing.

He spoke, "As with all stories, there are lessons to be learned from the errors of those who came before us. This story is no different. The Creator took the Flamethrowers away after a terrible tragedy that took the honor and respect away from the game. He banished the Guardians of the Game from their Nations."

Kenny was really curious now! *What could have happened to get the Creator to banish the Flamethrowers?* Kenny needed to know. This story was way too good to not know the whole thing.

"Sir, what happened to dishonor the game?" Kenny asked as softly and innocently as he could.

White Crane walked to the window that looked down upon the casino floor. Kenny watched as White Crane's long, flowing white robes touched the ground. He felt like he was in a dream - the white room, the white robes, and the old man with white hair standing in front of him.

White Crane then turned around and began, "The story is like many before it, a story of betrayal, deceit, and death. The proud Nation of the Snake had a great warrior named Silver Tongue. Silver Tongue was taught by his father to be a great warrior, and was expected to be his Nation's Flamethrower some day. One day, he grew jealous of the Bison Nation, seeing their great prairie lands and resources. Silver Tongue fell in love with the Bison chief's daughter and became obsessed with her. He knew he needed to defeat the Bison Nation to get her. Impatient to become the Flamethrower of his own Nation, Silver Tongue deceived and killed his Nation's Flamethrower. He lied to his elders that the Bison Nation had killed their leader. He claimed he was the rightful heir of the stick, and that a challenge must be made to the Bison Nation for their murderous ways."

"The Snake Nation elders did not know if they should believe the story about deceit by the Bison Nation. Silver Tongue used the hate-filled words of jealousy and hatred towards the Bison Nation to fill the hearts of the Snake Nation with fear and anger. The Bison Nation told the Snake Nation they did no such killing, and a game would not resolve this lie. But to honor the game, they had to accept the challenge from the Snake Nation. The Snake Nation traveled to the Bison Nation to make preparations for the game. But, Silver Tongue had no intention of playing the game."

"As the Nations lined up to begin the game, there were three hundred warriors on each side. As the ball was thrown into the air to begin the game, Silver Tongue took the spear he had hidden in his stick and pierced the heart of the Bison Flamethrower. Bison warriors were stunned seeing this attack. But suddenly each Snake Nation warrior also had hidden spears, and each killed their opponent quickly. And with that, the Snake Nation had killed the Bison Nation's best three hundred warriors in a few short minutes. Then Silver Tongue ran towards the Bison sidelines. His warriors followed him, spearing and killing the entire Bison Nation, except for the one woman he wanted."

"The Creator was angry at what Silver Tongue had done to one of his Nations. Using his game to deceive, betray, and kill an entire Nation. The Creator banned the Flamethrowers from their Nations and hid the sticks in stone boxes. The Creator promised some day he would return the Flamethrowers to the Nations and restore The Creators Game."

Kenny and Casey sat in silence, knowing this was an amazing story that not many people had the opportunity to hear. Kenny was amazed that the Storyteller would share this story of tragedy. Kenny felt humble that he had found the stick. *But why now? Why me?* He needed to ask.

Finally Kenny asked, "Why me, why now?"

White Crane looked puzzled, like he had the same questions. "Kenny, I do not claim to know the answers to those questions. I can only tell you what has happened in the past. These stories were told to me by my grandfather and his before him. We do not know how long ago these stories were made."

"What am I suppose to do with it?" asked Kenny.

"Again, I am not the one who should tell you what to do," answered White Crane.

"My stick looks like an owl. Does this mean this stick belonged to the Owl Nation?" asked Kenny.

White Crane answered, "Yes, the Owl Nation was a great and strong Nation."

Kenny looked puzzled, "Was?"

White Crane explained, "After the Flamethrowers were removed, many Nations faltered. Some merged, some lost their lands, and felt cursed by the Creator."

"I'm sorry, I didn't know," said Kenny humbly.

"We have many sad stories," explained White Crane.

Kenny and Casey watched as White Crane paced again. He then walked toward the windows, adding, "Did you find anything else in the cave?"

Kenny looked at Casey, "Did you see anything else?"

She shook her head no.

"Sir, I don't think we saw anything else, but we were pretty excited once we opened the stone box."

White Crane then explained, "The Flamethrowers true weapon of power is a red rock that is used to create tremendous fear in an opponent. No force on earth can stop the Flamethrower's rock."

Kenny questioned, "Red rock?"

"Yes, the red rock is a weapon that can only be used by the Flamethrower. This power allowed the Flame-thrower to control a situation and allowed the Flameth-rower to rule over his warriors. No one dared to challenge a Flamethrower in battle, for fear of this wea-pon. The legends say the rocks were to be buried near each stick. So when the sticks are returned, the power of the Flamethrower will also be returned."

Kenny was excited. *A weapon? A rock?* He wanted to go right back to the cave and look for it. Casey was sit-ting next to him thinking, *what just happened? Who is this guy? Why is he telling Kenny he's some next great warrior?* Something just didn't make sense to her.

Kenny, on the other hand, had no such suspicions. He was so excited that he thanked the Storyteller and started quickly for the door.

Legend

White Crane called out, "Kenny, you do not want to forget your new stick!"

Kenny beamed and thanked him again for everything.

As Kenny walked out of the casino, his feet barely touched the ground. He was so excited to go back to the cave.

Casey, half-jogging to keep up with him, said, "We need to tell everyone what happened, and the story."

Kenny looked surprised. "Would you believe me if I told *you* that story? We need to get back to the cave and find these red rocks! *Then* we can tell everyone. We can show them."

10

Trapped

Kenny was glad it was summer and there was no school. He couldn't imagine having to go to school and waiting all day to go back to the cave, back to the place where the Storyteller said he could find the weapon of the Flamethrowers. To find the red rocks.

Casey was nervous about going back to the cave, and was still feeling some jealously over the fact that the stick was real but only worked for Kenny. *Maybe all the sticks were buried in the same spot. Maybe in the same cave. Maybe there was one in there for me?* This idea drove Casey to join Kenny as he went back into the cave.

They were prepared like before, with flashlights, ropes, and other basic items, but this time they did not have his brother's cell phone. Kenny had brought a backpack to carry a few of the rocks he hoped to find. He didn't know how many there would be. A backpack seemed liked a good idea to him. Kenny kept thinking, *red rocks. But the cave was full of red rocks, because of the iron ore in the soil. Everything was a dirty red.*

Kenny led the way confidently. This was his third time in the cave this week. They reached the stone box. It was still there, but now it was closed. *Had someone closed it? Or did something happen to make it close?*

"Casey, did we close the stone box when we left last time?" asked Kenny.

"I don't remember. We left in such a hurry."

Kenny knew that was true. "Okay let's split up and look around."

Casey glared at him. "Kenny we are not splitting up. What if something happens to one of us? We need to stay together. We need to stay safe."

"We can go faster if we split up," explained Kenny,

who was excited to find the rocks.

"No, I am not leaving you alone, Kenny," she insisted.

Kenny wanted to find the rocks, so this was not the time to argue. He reluctantly agreed, and they started deeper into the cave. There were lots of choices. There were so many tunnels to go down. Casey carefully marked each one by carving an X at the entrance of each tunnel as they entered it.

To Casey, it seemed like they'd been in the cave for hours. But Kenny would not give up. Casey started to get tired and said, "Kenny we need to take a break. I am getting tired and we have been down so many tunnels. Let's go out and take a break. We can sit down and think about this. Think about where they could be."

"Casey, you can go back, but I'm going to keep looking. It's okay, I'll be fine," said Kenny.

Casey knew better. She could not leave Kenny alone in the cave. She knew he was so focused on the rocks he'd lose track of the tunnels and get lost. After begging and begging, Casey finally got Kenny to agree to leave the cave and take a break.

As they were walking back it hit Casey. *The rocks would be buried in the same room as the stick, right? The person would have put them close by or left a clue there.* But she waited to say anything to Kenny until they got outside.

As they walked out of the cave, they were surprised and startled to find several teenagers from the Nation. At first Kenny thought they just wanted to see the stick or something. The Storyteller must have told them about it. But Kenny would find out very quickly this was not their intent.

One the young men yelled to Kenny, "That stick belongs to our Nation! It is not yours! You must return it!"

Kenny knew the Storyteller had said it was his, but they were outnumbered ten to two. Kenny was getting nervous. He needed to buy some time.

Kenny calmly said, "I found the stick and it has bonded to me. The stick belongs to me now. Ask the Storyteller, he will tell you."

Kenny noticed that Casey had moved behind him.

Another from the group yelled back, "The old man has no idea what he's talking about. He is too old to understand that the stick belongs to the Nation, not you! Give it back and we will not hurt you."

Kenny felt they were serious; their eyes were intensely focused on Kenny.

Kenny hesitated, then decided to stand his ground.

"The stick will only work for me. Its powers are limited to only me. It will do you no good."

The leader of the group, Ron, glared at Kenny, "I'm sure the old man told you how the power of stick is transferred to the next person."

They boys all laughed.

"We know how to get the power of the stick for ourselves. You don't need to worry about us."

Casey knew there was only one option to keep the stick and that was to run back into the cave. She saw they had no flashlights. *We could easily lose them inside,* she thought. Casey looked at Kenny and motioned to the cave as discretely as she could.

Kenny noticed they were only about five steps from the entrance. Kenny took a slow step back towards the cave. Casey moved as if shadowing him.

The teenagers cried out, "Do not run, Kenny! Yes, we know who you are, and we will find you."

Kenny and Casey both hesitated now. *Had these boys been in the casino? Had they followed them? How did they know their names?*

"Casey, run for it," Kenny yelled. They both turned and ran frantically into the cave.

The boys ran after them.

Kenny knew the turns and as they ran he fumbled with the flashlight, trying to get some light into the suddenly lightless cave.

"Kenny, no! Turn off your flashlight!" gasped Casey.

The flashlight went out and she grabbed Kenny and they stopped and tried hard to quiet their breathing.

The teenagers had followed but now could only see the small light from the opening of the cave. They had nothing to follow and could hear nothing.

"We're going to lose them!" called out one.

"We can't see, we do not have any lights," said another.

Ron confidently said, "They aren't going anywhere. We will wait for them outside!"

Ron called out to Kenny, "We will be waiting for you Kenny! You have nowhere to go. The stick will be ours soon."

The teenagers turned to leave the cave, heckling Kenny and Casey as they left.

Kenny and Casey stood as quietly as they could for a few minutes. Their hearts were pounding and it sounded loud in their heads. Casey was now holding Kenny and she awkwardly let go.

Kenny wondered, *would they really kill me for the*

power of the stick? Was this really happening?

Casey knew they needed to find another way out of the cave. But he still wanted to find the red rocks. *Maybe the rocks would show them a way out,* he thought.

Casey turned on her flashlight. "Kenny, I was thinking that the rocks should be near where we found the stick. We didn't check that room very closely. We should go back and start there."

Kenny nodded in agreement.

But they were both scared and worried about what would happen next.

Despite the fear, Kenny felt he had to find the rocks. Something was making him feel that the rocks would save them.

Kenny led Casey back to the room where they'd found the stone box.

They started looking very closely around the dark room.

"Look for markings like the owl on the walls," she suggested.

Kenny put the flashlight in his mouth and started feeling and searching along the wall for stone shapes. He dug dirt from the walls, trying to find something he recognized.

Casey did the same and they worked their way around the room. As they got closer to each other, they realized they had covered the entire room and had found nothing.

Casey was dejected. She was sure the rocks would be in this room. Kenny could see Casey was really disappointed.

"Casey, it's okay. It was a good idea. It made sense. Let's think about it some more."

The flashlights were starting to dim.

"Kenny, we should turn off the flashlights. We need to save the batteries."

They both sat down and turned off the flashlights.

The room became pitch black. They couldn't see anything at all.

Kenny sat there, wondering if he'd become too obsessed with everything. No matter how brave she was acting, Kenny suspected Casey was nervous. He thought, *what if we just leave the cave and give the stick to the boys. Maybe I could get it back later.*

He felt he had to make sure Casey was going to be safe, even though he knew she could take care of herself. He'd gotten her into this, and he had to make sure he could get her out safely. She was a true friend. She

111

went to the casino, and inside the cave, even though she didn't want to. What was he going to do?

While sitting there in the blackness, Kenny pulled the Flamethrower stick out of the backpack. As his hand wrapped around the stick, it began to glow as before. Kenny noticed that as the glow from the stick got brighter, a glow began to appear through the wall.

"Casey!" he whispered excitedly. "Look! The wall is glowing!

Kenny let go of the stick to touch the wall, but the glow disappeared.

"Kenny, you have to keep holding it. They're connected somehow," she said.

Kenny held the stick near the wall, and Casey started to brush dirt from the wall. After several minutes, they found a small door in the rock wall.

"Casey, you were right!" yelled Kenny.

As they peeled away the dirt, owl markings became clear, even in the dim light. Casey and Kenny, using one hand, worked hard to clear the dirt. They were filthy now.

"Do you see a door knob or handle or anything?" asked Kenny.

"No," answered Casey with a frustrated tone.

They looked carefully but could not see a way to open the stone door.

Casey looked at Kenny and asked, "How did you open the box? Do you remember?"

Kenny thought for a moment. "We twisted the owl's head using the eyes!"

They both looked hard, but there were no eyes on the stone door. They looked around and could not find anything that was a hole or area to twist. This was supposed to be their way out. They just had to find a way to open the door.

She told Kenny, "Move the stick all along the door and look for something that moves or glows brighter than the other areas."

As he moved the stick around the stone door, it did glow stronger.

Casey stepped back as Kenny moved it around the door again.

"Kenny, stop. Now move the stick towards the door and twist to your right."

Casey was seeing a pattern from the glow where the stick might fit.

"Stop. Now push the stick and touch the stone door."

As he did so, the stone door grew brighter. But while

the door grew brighter, it remained shut.

"Now what, Casey?" he asked.

She thought for a few moments. "Do you think you should turn the stick like a handle? Will it move to the left or right?"

Kenny kept the stick against the door and tried twisting to the right, but nothing happened. It didn't move. Next he moved it to the left.

This time, they both heard a familiar CLICK.

"You did it, Kenny!" she cried.

A handle appeared on the wall.

They each put a hand on the handle and looked at each other.

"Pull," they said softly to each other.

The door moved only slightly.

"Pull harder," they said together and louder.

The door opened far enough for them to grab the door and move it all the way open after considerable effort.

The stone door was very heavy and very cold. As they looked inside, there was only one thing they could see...*steps*. And they appeared to go straight up.

"You ready to go?" asked Kenny.

"Yeah," answered Casey, "Use your stick to light the

way and we'll save the flashlights for later."

Kenny took the first step and looked up. He could see nothing but more steps in front of him. It was going to be a long climb.

11

Red Rocks

Kenny started up the stone steps and Casey followed closely behind. There was very little head room; the steps were so steep it was difficult to move very quickly. Kenny used the stick to light the way.

Unfortunately, the light failed to go very far, and they became focused on just going from step to step. Kenny started counting as he went, but got distracted several times and lost track.

The stone steps were sturdy and as Kenny looked closely at some of them, they appeared to have the im-

116

ages of an owl imprinted on them. Whoever built these stone boxes, doors, and steps certainly spent a lot of time and took some pride in building them. Kenny wondered if an Owl Flamethrower had been the builder. The Storyteller didn't say how the stone boxes were built. He hadn't mentioned there would be a stone door. *Maybe he didn't know himself,* thought Kenny.

Kenny was getting thirsty but he kept plodding upward. He checked once in a while to make sure Casey was close, and she always was, right there step-by-step with him. She was being very quiet. Kenny wondered how she was doing. He certainly had not made this easy on her.

Casey, on the other hand, was surprised that Kenny was still going. She knew that not much motivated Kenny in hockey, and he would give up easily at times when things got tough. But this was different. Kenny was focused and working hard. *He must really believe these stories from the Storyteller. And why not? They seem to fit. But really. Flamethrowers? Creator's game? Stone boxes? Stone doors? This was just becoming too crazy. Why did Kenny get the stick? Why didn't anyone else see the stone box before?*

Kenny paused for a moment, "Casey, you doing

okay?" He was hoping she needed a break.

"Yeah," she answered, "But I could use a breather."

"Sounds good," said Kenny, relieved.

As they stopped, Kenny started to apologize. "I'm sorry I got you into this mess. We shouldn't be in here alone with no cell phone to call anyone. I'm sure you're mad at me, but –"

Casey interrupted, seeing that he was sincere, "Hey, we're having a great adventure! We're going to have a great story to tell everyone."

Kenny smiled. Casey certainly knew him well.

"How much further you think we'll have to go?" she asked. "Can you see an end?"

Kenny held the stick up, but it didn't shed light beyond the next few steps.

"Kenny, let go of the stick for a minute." Casey suggested.

As Kenny let go of the stick, the stairway became very dark. But as their eyes adjusted, Kenny and Casey could see a small light from above.

"I think that's the sun up there," said Casey. "I think this must open at the top of the hill!"

Kenny was glad there was a way out, but he was also suddenly conflicted.

"Casey, what about the red rocks?" he asked.

"Kenny, we have to focus on getting out of the cave. There will be plenty of time to come back and bring others to help us. People are going to believe us now. We have a stone box, a stone door, and steps to show them. They have to believe you now."

Kenny knew Casey was right. They were both exhausted, and just getting out of the cave alive was a good enough goal for now.

"Okay, let's keep going up and get out of here," he finally said after a few moments.

He grabbed the stick again and they resumed their climb up the stone steps.

Kenny was moving a little quicker now that they could see a way out. As Kenny started to get closer to the top, he could see the light from the sun on the stone steps. But the closer he got, the more he realized that the opening was very small, maybe the size of basketball. Nothing he and Casey would easily fit through.

Kenny stopped as he reached the last step. "Casey, this is the last step, but the hole is not big enough for us to get through."

Casey squinted at it, thinking.

"We've gotta dig our way out," she said looking at

her hands. They were covered in dirt already from digging in the room and getting the stone door open.

She smiled and said, "Well, it's not like we're going to get any more dirty. You're gonna need a bath before you see your mom anyway, dude."

They laughed and started pulling the dirt away from the hole, making it wider. As Kenny tried to move the dirt farther from the opening, he felt the wall against him begin to give way.

He lost his balance, and as he fell backwards he called out, "Casey!"

She turned just as Kenny fell through the wall behind him. "Kenny!" she yelled as he disappeared.

The impact as he landed knocked the wind out of him. He remembered the time when Paul had tripped him in practice and he crashed back-first into the boards at full speed. He remembered the coach telling him to start with small, short breaths to get his wind back.

He started to hear Casey's voice now, "Kenny! Kenny! Are you okay?"

Kenny had landed on something very hard and very uneven. He yelled back up to Casey, "I'm okay. Just landed on something really hard and ..."

Kenny had dropped the stick, so there was no light.

He rolled over onto all fours so he could crawl around. The floor was very uneven; it even seemed to move as he did.

Casey found her flashlight and started shining it down into the area where Kenny fell.

She saw the stick and called out, "Kenny, the stick is to your right, about six feet."

Kenny turned to his left. "Your other right!" she called out, chuckling under her breath.

Kenny smiled and shook his head. Then he moved to his right. As he was moving, Casey saw that the ground below Kenny moved when he moved.

"Kenny, what's that you're crawling on? It looks like balls, like tennis balls."

Kenny stopped and realized she was right. He was crawling on tennis balls. But they weren't soft like tennis balls. He grabbed one and it felt as hard as stone.

Suddenly it dawned on him.

"Casey! Casey! These must be the rocks, the red rocks! They have to be!" Kenny continued to move towards the stick. Reaching with his hand he finally felt the stick with his hand. As he grabbed it, the stick lit up and he could see the red rocks.

It felt as heavy as a hockey puck and smooth like

one, too. Casey looked down and realized Kenny was about ten feet below her. There was no way down to him. She needed to find a way to get him out.

Kenny, of course, was focused on the red rocks.

"Casey, throw down my backpack!" Kenny yelled.

"Why?" she asked in a distracted voice. She was focused on how to get him out.

"Because I want to fill the backpack with the red rocks," he said with a tone of 'DUH!'

"Oh, yeah! So I have to pull you AND a backpack full of rocks out of there," she said sarcastically.

Kenny wasn't listening. He was focused on the red rocks. He picked up several more and inspected them. They all seemed about the same size and weight. But unlike the other items, these seemed to have no symbols or engravings on them at all. He had expected they would have an owl symbol or some other mark that tied them to the other things.

Casey tossed down the backpack after taking out the rope. Kenny grabbed the backpack and opened it quickly, putting some of the red rocks inside.

As he greedily filled the backpack, Casey realized she was not going to be able to pull him out by herself. She was going to need to anchor the rope to something.

Seeing nothing around her, she decided the best place might be a tree or large boulder outside the cave.

Casey resumed digging at the opening. It was almost large enough already. She pulled a bit more dirt away, and soon there was a large enough area that she thought she could get through. She moved over to where Kenny had fallen.

"Kenny, I'm dropping a rope down to you. Don't pull on it yet. I need to find something to tie it to. I will yell down when I'm ready."

Casey climbed through the hole. The sun was blinding to her. It was late afternoon and the heat from the sun felt good. She hadn't realized how cold it was inside the cave. As her eyes adjusted to the sun, she saw trees nearby. *Cool* ! she thought. *I'll tie this end around the tree and he can pull himself up.*

After she finished tying the rope off she leaned over the hole and yelled down to Kenny, "Okay the rope is ready, pull yourself up!" Then she tugged on the rope.

Kenny felt the rope get pulled on. He couldn't quite hear everything she said, but he got the idea. He picked up the backpack. It was really heavy, loaded down with rocks. Kenny felt the backpack really weighing him down. He thought to himself, *okay this is going to be tough, but I need these rocks. I can take these back to the Storyteller.* He even wondered if he could get a few more into the bag.

Kenny grabbed the rope and started to pull himself up and used his feet to walk up the wall. The wall was uneven, and he was able to find holds for his feet. Slowly he worked his way up.

Casey was calling down to him, giving him instructions and encouragement. He motioned for her to take the backpack so he could pull himself out of the opening.

Casey tried to hoist the backpack, but she could only get it to clear the hole, then it dropped to the ground beside her with a clanking sound. "Geez Kenny, how many rocks did you put in this thing?"

"Casey, we did it! We made it out and we got the rocks!" he said triumphantly. He was lying on the ground beside the backpack, surprised how tired he suddenly felt.

"Yeah, well I suspect our friends are still waiting near our bikes," said Casey.

Kenny got up slowly. His arms were sore, his back was sore, he was exhausted.

He bent over and slowly snuck over to a spot where

he could look down the hill. He could not see them at first, but he could hear voices. They were still down there. They were still sitting just outside the entrance to the cave, talking.

Kenny crawled back over to Casey. "Yup, still there. We need another plan." Kenny was just so exhausted. So was Casey. Thinking up an escape plan – and carrying it out – was more than they wanted to deal with right now. But they also knew they had to do something.

Kenny crawled over to the backpack and unzipped it. He wanted to look more closely at the rocks.

He reached in and pulled out one of the rocks. As he held the rock, Kenny thought, *this is about as heavy as a hockey puck, very smooth but not shiny.*

He held the rock up towards the sun to see if he could see through it. No. It was a solid red color. He rubbed his hand over it and thought, *could it be rubber? plastic? What was it made of that it could it be so perfectly round, smooth, and colorful? How could this be the great weapon of the Flamethrowers?*

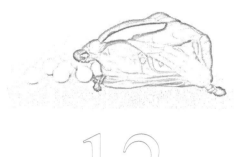

Fireballs

Casey and Kenny sat on top of the hill for several minutes catching their breath. Down below were the teenage boys who had followed them to the cave and trapped them.

Casey, regaining her strength, had an idea. "Kenny, we need to create a distraction so we can get down the hill, get our bikes, and get out of here."

"Sounds good," he said. "What kinda distraction do you have in mind?"

"We could throw some rocks down the other side of the hill and get them to think we found another way out over there. Then we could run down to our bikes," she said.

"Ok, but we need to stay low so they don't see us. We need to be very quiet," added Kenny.

They started to move slowly across the top of the hill, crouched down as far as they could. As they reached the far side of the hill, Casey and Kenny picked up some rocks.

Casey whispered over to Kenny, "Try and throw against those large rocks. They will think we found a way out over there."

They quickly stood up and threw several rocks each, hitting the large rocks.

The boys below reacted immediately.

"Did you hear that?" asked one.

"Do you see anyone?" asked another.

"Did they find another way out?" said Ron.

The boys started to move towards the large rocks on the far side of the hill. As they started to move away, Kenny and Casey started back towards the other side, where their bikes were.

Kenny moved carefully, trying not to make any noise and keep out of sight. Slowly, Casey followed behind. As she moved behind Kenny, she could feel the dirt under her left foot start to give way. She quickly moved her weight back to her right foot and clutched at the grasses around her. *That was close,* she thought, her heart pounding. Kenny turned back to see her clinging to the hill.

He offered, "Be careful Casey, the dirt is loose in some spots." *Yeah, great time to tell me, after I almost fell* she grumbled to herself.

The boys reached the large rocks and started to look around. They didn't see an opening out of the cave or any sign of Kenny or Casey.

The boys start arguing about where the noise might have come from.

Kenny and Casey kept making their way across the hillside, and were almost back to where the backpack and stick were. Casey continued to have problems with the soft dirt, and after planting her left foot on a small rock, the rock gave way and started rolling down the hill.

"Down!" gasped Kenny in alarm. "Get down!"

But it was too late; one of the boys looked up the hill and saw them.

"There they are, up there!" he said, pointing directly up at Kenny and Casey.

Kenny was frozen for a moment, but Casey was beginning to slide further down the hill. She was exhausted and her strength was beginning to leave her.

She reached and tried to grab onto grass, branches, anything to slow her down. Finally, she managed to hold onto some small rocks that stuck out of the hillside. But she knew she could not make a move back up the hill. She was stuck.

The boys made their way back to right below Casey, and started walking up the hill. They had been waiting a long time and were determined to get the stick.

They were hiking up the hill fast, straight for Casey, who was clinging to the small rocks on the hillside.

Kenny was getting scared and started to panic.

How am I going to save Casey and keep the stick? What should I do? What would they do to Casey?

Kenny pushed the questions out of his head. *Okay, what do I have to help me? The backpack!*

He ran over to the backpack and opened it up. He grabbed one of the red rocks and threw it in the general direction of the boys. "Leave her alone! It's me you want."

Kenny then grabbed the stick and held it up for them to see.

Ron saw the stick and called out, "The stick is ours

Kenny, throw it down here and we'll go."

The boys were moving towards Kenny now. He had distracted them for the moment away from Casey.

Kenny grabbed another rock from the bag. This time he placed it in the stick. As soon as he did, he noticed that the rock started to glow. Changing from a red, the rock became brighter and brighter orange, as if it was actually getting hot.

Kenny stared in shock as the rock grew brighter and then suddenly, BANG, the rock caught fire. Kenny was startled and dropped the stick to the ground.

As the stick hit the ground, the burning rock suddenly went back to the color of red, and was no longer on fire. Kenny looked at the ball and the stick puzzled. *What is going on? What kind of –.*

"Kenny!" yelled Casey, "I can't hold on much longer. I'm gonna fall!"

It was at that moment that Kenny realized what the Storyteller had been telling him. The red rocks were the weapon of the Flamethrowers! They had special powers with the stick!

Kenny yelled back, "Hold on Casey! I figured out the red rocks! I got it!"

Kenny picked up the stick. He knew what to do. He

had a power with these rocks. He could scare these guys away.

Kenny stood up and confidently put the red rock back in the stick. The rock started to glow and then, BANG, the rock caught fire. He was ready to shoot now. He aimed right in front of Ron, who was moving up the hill. BAM! The flaming rock hit right in front of Ron, knocking him back.

"What the hell was that?" yelled one of the boys.

Kenny was now standing proud on top of the hill, with another rock glowing in the stick. BANG, it caught fire and he threw it right across the front of another boy, knocking him to the ground.

The rocks seemed to explode as they hit the ground, causing great damage to the hillside and sending lots of dirt into the air.

Kenny picked up another rock. He held up the stick and said in a strong, confident voice, "I haven't aimed for you guys yet. This would really hurt if it actually hit you. It's time to leave, Ron."

Kenny knew Casey needed his help, and he had to quickly get them out of there so he could help her.

Ron stood up, moving forward again and ignoring Kenny's warning. Kenny saw that Ron was not ready to give up.

Kenny held on to the rock longer this time. He looked at the stick and wondered *why doesn't the stick catch fire?*

Kenny fired the next shot right behind Ron, knocking him down again. The rock created a huge hole in the side of the hill.

Kenny realized a rock gained more power the longer he held it in the Flamethrower stick.

Ron was hurt now; his leg had been burned from the last shot.

Bleeding and in pain, he called out to his friends, "Let's get out of here!"

Ron glared up at Kenny and angrily yelled, "This is not over Kenny! We will get that stick from you!"

Kenny looked over, and Casey was barely hanging on. He ran towards her and reached down the hill with the stick.

"Grab on, I'll pull you up!" he said.

Casey let go of the clump of rocks she was holding onto and grabbed the stick. Kenny used his weight and leaned back to pull her up. Casey was able to climb up to a safer spot on the hillside.

"What just happened, Kenny?" she pleaded. "I

couldn't see much and there were fireballs coming down the hill!"

"I figured out what the red rocks do, Casey. They are the weapons of the stick. They catch fire and become a weapon you can throw," said Kenny.

"The red rocks seem to have special powers when they are placed in the Flamethrower stick. The name Flamethrowers seems to make more sense now. They literally throw fireballs."

Casey and Kenny made their way down the hill to their bikes. There was no sign of any of the boys, so they headed for home.

Family and Friends

Kenny got to his front door and paused, looked down at himself. He was covered in dirt and sweat.

He stepped back off the porch and wiped off all the loose dirt he could. He removed his shirt and wiped his face. *Can't let mom see me this dirty,* he thought. He walked over to the bench on the porch and hid the stick behind it. Kenny wasn't ready to show his family the stick. Not yet.

Kenny walked into the house. Sure enough, mom

started in right away.

"Where have you been?" she demanded. "I told you to be home by three to help me with –." Her eyes widened, now seeing Kenny in full view. "You look filthy! What in the world were you doing? Go take a shower and clean up this instant."

Kenny was happy to go take a shower. He had asked Casey to come over after dinner, and they would talk about what to do next. So much had happened!

Kenny was finishing dinner when Casey walked in.

"Hey Casey," said Kenny's mom.

"Hi Mrs. C," she responded.

"Casey," said Ryan, "I need some help tomorrow with the mites at camp. You and Kenny want to help out?"

Casey always liked an excuse to skate, but she was really distracted.

She reluctantly said, "I don't know, Ryan. I'm not feeling all that great." Everyone turned and looked at her, shocked. Casey never turned down a chances to skate.

Kenny's mom asked, "You feeling okay Casey?"

Kenny looked at Casey, worried she might say something.

Casey looked down and said, "I'm really tired right now; I was really looking forward to sleeping in tomorrow."

Ryan volleyed back, "Not a problem! The little guys don't start until one in the afternoon. I'll see you then." Ryan, not letting her think of any more excuses, walked out of the room.

Casey and Kenny headed downstairs to talk.

"Casey, how much of this story do you think is true?" asked Kenny.

"The Storyteller was right about the red rocks being there," said Casey. "I don't think anyone would go to all this trouble to try and make us believe. But, I don't know how much of it is really true."

"Do you think there are really other sticks like this buried out there? Other animals, like he talked about?" asked Kenny.

Casey answered, "I have no idea. I am still working on the whole 'this stick exists' thing. Hey wait, where's the stick?"

Kenny held up his hand as if to say 'hold on.' He had forgotten he'd left it on the porch. He bounded up the stairs and out of sight, then returned to the basement with it.

Casey and Kenny examined the stick again. It looked so old and yet was in such great condition.

"Who do think could make a stick like this? How long would it take? And why don't the strings catch on fire?" Kenny was just rambling out questions.

Casey was just as puzzled; she pulled out one of the red rocks and looked at it. "The Storyteller only said these were weapons of the Flamethrower. He didn't say they caught fire or were used to destroy things. He must not have told us everything."

Kenny nodded in agreement, "We have to go back and see him again."

Casey had a concerned look on her face, "What if we run into Ron and his friends again?"

"We need to talk to him again," insisted Kenny, "We need to know the whole story."

"Well, I guess this answers our first question. We must believe him," said Casey.

Kenny smiled. There seemed to be no other explanation for where the stick was from and how the rocks worked.

Casey asked, "Have you told anyone else about the stick?"

Kenny reassured her, "Not since the park when I showed it off. I'm not sure anyone is really ready to believe us. Do you think Paul or Frank would believe us now?"

Casey shook her head no. She knew it was a tough story to believe. Flamethrowers, guardians of the game, developed by the Creator.

"Kenny, we could use someone to go with us to see the Storyteller. Even if Frank doesn't believe us, he would be good to tag along. He's big and would make me feel better if we ran into Ron."

Kenny nodded okay, and added, "That's actually a good idea. Frank's brother has an old truck and he can probably give us a ride, too."

Kenny walked upstairs to call Frank. Casey followed, and when Kenny hung up he said, "We're all set. We should get some rest, it's gonna be a long day. Meet me here at 8."

The next morning Kenny and Casey hopped in the truck with Frank and his older brother. Kenny thanked him for the ride. He showed Frank the red rocks he brought with him, but he had left the stick at home so it wouldn't be taken in case Ron and his friends were there.

They arrived at the casino and Little Joe was there again out front. There was no sign of Ron or his friends. Little Joe saw them and smiled, "White Crane said you would be back to see him soon. I see he was right. I Ie said to bring you right up when you arrived."

Little Joe escorted them up to the top of the casino, just as he did before. He knocked on the white door. White Crane opened the door and welcomed them in.

"I see you brought a new friend with you this time."

Kenny answered, "We had some trouble with a guy named Ron who wanted the stick from me. Frank's here to help even up the numbers."

White Crane smiled, and turned to Kenny, "Ron is the son of the current tribal leader. He knows the legend well and I'm sure he feels he is entitled to the stick of the Owl, not you."

"How did he find out about it?" asked Kenny.

White Crane knew the real reason for asking, "I did not send him, if that's what you mean Kenny. You walked right up to this casino with the stick in your hand. Little Joe delivered it to me in front of many tribal leaders. The whole Nation knows you have the stick by now," then added, "I see you did not bring the stick."

Kenny looked at Casey and answered, "We thought it best not to tempt anyone."

Casey smiled.

Kenny reached into his backpack and brought out

one of the red rocks. "We did find the red rocks."

White Crane walked slowly over to Kenny and looked at the red rock. He looked at Kenny, who nodded that it was okay to take it. White Crane took the rock and rubbed his hand slowly over the stone's smooth surface. He held it up and turned it slowly, inspecting it very carefully.

He finally spoke. "I take it you put this in the stick."

Kenny nodded, waiting to see if White Crane would explain more, now that he knew Kenny had figured out the secret of the rocks.

White Crane turned and walked to his desk. "Have a seat my friends. There is more to the story that you need to know."

Kenny smiled. He knew White Crane had not told them the whole story.

Casey, Frank, and Kenny took a seat on the white couch. The old man leaned against his desk and looked up slightly, as if to find a place in his mind to start the story.

Meanwhile...

Briggs awoke in his trailer. He looked out the window

140

and saw that vandals had once again broken into the mine. Briggs followed the trail of footprints into the west shaft. The footprints came to an end. But there was no one there. Another break in. *What are they looking for?* thought Briggs. Nothing seems to be missing or damaged.

Balance of Power

White Crane was leaning on his desk ready to tell Casey, Frank, and Kenny more about the Flamethrower story. He had paused because Kenny had given him something he had never seen before, a red rock. Not just any red rock, but the weapon of the Flamethrowers.

He began, but with a warning. "Friends, our Nation has told these stories since the beginning. We do not write down these stories. Instead they are repeated at important events so everyone will know and remember their meaning. They are the most sacred of our stories. I have not shared these with others outside our Nation so

142

you must listen well and understand what I am about to say. You may not understand everything. That is to be expected. But you must respect these stories for what they are, a history of our Nation."

Casey and Kenny looked at each other and then Frank. Frank was now on the edge of his seat. *This is getting good*, he thought. The three of them nodded their vow back to White Crane.

"I mentioned before that the Flamethrowers were the guardians of the game, being blessed with the Flamethrower sticks. Each Nation had their own animal, and sticks to match those animals. The Flamethrowers were the inspirational leaders of their Nation. The Flamethrowers held a special bond in turning young warriors into men. Flamethrowers coached the young men in the ways of respect, honor, and playing the game. They taught them about the Creator, their Nation's animal, and to take pride in their Nation."

White Crane turned and started to pace. "As Nations competed over the years, the Flamethrowers would have conflicts with outsiders or other Nations that needed to be resolved. Games were often used to resolve these conflicts. But if a Nation did not follow the rules or cheated, the Flamethrower's job was to enforce the rules."

"Eventually the Creator granted the Flamethrowers a weapon of special rocks that were to enforce the rules. These rocks, as you have noticed, have special powers. They can glow or even catch on fire, to be thrown at an enemy to scare them or injure them."

White Crane turned to Kenny. "I heard that Ron was injured during your encounter at the cave."

Kenny gulped and was about to say something in his defense, but White Crane continued, "No worries. I'm sure he deserved it."

White Crane moved toward the windows overlooking the casino. "Our stories have been passed down from generation to generation. Sometimes, details get confused. To be honest, I was not sure the rocks actually existed. I was not sure they really caught fire. But I heard from Ron's father what had been witnessed."

White Crane returned to his story. "The Flamethrowers took their role as leaders of young men very seriously. They were the best men in their Nation and trained their warriors well. Most Flamethrowers were strong and fierce men, with the courage to train and teach the young men how to be good men. But as you know, it was jealously that brought them down."

Now White Crane started pacing faster around the room. Casey could tell there was something more he was not yet telling them.

Kenny stood up and moved around the white table in front of him. "Is there something else?" Kenny asked White Crane quietly.

White Crane looked at Kenny, "There is something you must know, must understand."

After what felt like several minutes, he returned to the story. "As with all things made by the Creator, there is a light and a dark. There are rules even the Creator must follow. All things in harmony."

Kenny, thinking he understood, started to say, "We know you mentioned Silver Tongue, and how he used the stick for evil, and killed the Nation of the Bison."

White Crane looked down, "I'm afraid I did not tell you the whole story the first time."

Frank sat up now and, smiling, whispered to Casey, "This is getting good!"

"Silver Tongue did not get his power from the Snake Nation's Flamethrower stick."

Casey and Kenny looked puzzled. They were not following. *What other item could be more powerful than the stick?*

"As I said before, the Creator must follow the rules of the universe, too. When he created the Flamethrower stick for good, he was forced to create one for evil as well."

It was becoming clearer to Kenny now. There were two sticks, not one that could be both good and evil, but two separate sticks.

White Crane continued, "Each Nation was given one Flamethrower stick and one evil stick. The good stick has all that is good about the animal and the Nation inside it. The evil stick has all the bad qualities of the animal and the Nation as its source of power. The sticks are of equal strength and power. In harmony. But, the person who holds the evil stick - no matter how good they may be - the evil in the stick will possess them. It will control them and their actions."

Casey asked, "So when you told us that Silver Tongue killed to get the Flamethrower stick, he had actually found the evil stick of the Snake Nation, and it possessed him?"

White Crane nodded and confirmed her idea.

"Yes, the Flamethrower of the Snake Nation had failed to protect his people from the evil stick, and it was found by Silver Tongue. With the evil stick, he was able to kill the Flamethrower of his Nation and to challenge the Bison Nation and destroy them."

Frank was now really interested in the story and started to ask questions, too. "How did the Flamethrowers keep it away from the people? Was it his job to keep it safe?"

"Of course the Flamethrowers knew of the evil stick, but never spoke of it so they would not tempt anyone to look for it. The Flamethrower would pass on both sticks, but the evil stick would always remain locked up in the stone tomb that had been created for it," said White Crane.

Frank continued asking questions, "Why did the Creator have to create an evil stick? I mean he is all powerful, right?"

Casey decided to answer for him. "Frank, all religions include a good and evil side of all things. We are Christian and we have Jesus and Satan. It's the order of things. It's the balance of things. The Chinese call it the Yin and the Yang. The black and the white, the light and the dark. All things in balance and harmony."

White Crane smiled at her and turned to Kenny with instructions. "You must locate the evil stick and its stone box. BUT, you must not open the box. Do not reveal it to anyone. The evil stick is not to be touched and must be kept secret. Only the Flamethrowers know this secret. When you find the evil stick you must protect it."

Kenny's mind was numb. He looked at Casey and Frank in shock.

Frank was ready to question White Crane, though. "Dude, how are we going to find this evil stick? I mean, how do you know the one Kenny already found was not the evil one?"

Kenny looked at Frank, Casey too. She was shocked at what seemed to be an accusation, and jumped to Kenny's defense. "How can you say Kenny found the evil one?" she demanded.

White Crane interrupted, "You would not be here if the one you found was evil. You will know what it looks like because it will be similar in style to the one you found with owls on it, but it will be darker. The stone box will have a large red mark warning anyone not to open it. The owl will look angry, as if to show the hatred that is inside. Remember, it will turn anyone who touches the stick to an evil person. No matter who you are. Casey, Frank, you cannot touch the stick or open the stone box. Do you understand?" Casey and Frank looked at each other, then back at White Crane. They nodded.

Kenny watched as White Crane walked towards him, returning the red rock. "You must find it first, and quickly. The Flamethrowers were supposed to, according to legend, bury the evil stick near the Flamethrower stick, only deeper in the ground, to always guarantee the Flamethrower stick would be found first. But I cannot tell for sure that is where the evil stick is located."

He leaned forward and looked at Kenny. "For whatever reason, Kenny, you have been chosen for this stick. You are now a Flamethrower, and you have duties to perform. You must locate the evil stick as soon as possible. Then protect it."

Kenny was feeling overwhelmed now, and confused. The stick was great and all, but what were all these responsibilities? Was he trapped by the stick now? He looked up and asked a simple question.

"Why me? I mean, why someone like me, who was never part of the Owl Nation, or played the game? I mean, how can I be the guardian of a game I've never played? This doesn't make any sense."

Casey and Frank nodded their heads in agreement. Why would Kenny be forced to take on this role as Flamethrower and play some role in the Nation?

"Kenny," said White Crane, "After our Flamethrowers

were removed from the earth, many Nations did not survive on their own. Most Nations merged together, sometimes to help one another, other times to try and survive the invasions that pushed them from their lands. I was originally from the Crane Nation, but we merged with the Owl Nation and others. Not everyone even knows the original Nation they were born into. With that said, we do not know why the Creator has chosen you, or what is going to happen as the other sticks are found. The stories only refer to the idea that the Flamethrowers will return to the earth and restore order to the Nations."

Kenny was still overwhelmed. *How can I take on this job? Who am I to do this?*

White Crane, sensing Kenny's concerns, simply said one last thing, "Kenny, you will be guided by the powers of the Flamethrower before you. Each stick carries the power and knowledge of those who held it before you. It is said you will have them as a guide throughout the rest of your life. Listen to the stick. And that is all I can tell you." He nodded towards the door letting them know they needed to begin their important task.

With that Casey, Frank, and Kenny walked towards the door. Kenny turned and, trying to reassure White

Crane that they understood their task, added, "Don't worry. We will not let you down."

As they exited the casino, Casey looked at the time. "Kenny! It's almost one! We have to get to the rink! We're going to be late for your brother's clinic!"

Kenny asked, "Should we blow off the clinic and go back to the cave?"

Casey looked at him and scolded, "You know your family, Kenny. You would be grounded, and we can't afford for you to be grounded. We have to look for the stick. Tomorrow."

Still, Kenny wondered, "What if someone finds it before us?"

"Dude, its been buried for centuries. And nobody else knows about it. I think you have time," Frank added with a touch of authority. "I'll go with you to the clinic and we can figure out a plan to go find it."

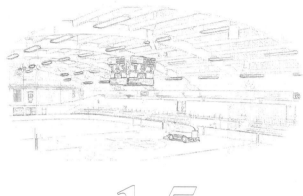

Grounded

They arrived at the rink about thirty minutes late and Ryan was not happy. Casey, Frank, and Kenny all helped at the clinic, but Ryan would not let it go.

"You had all morning to sleep in or do whatever it is you do and you couldn't get here on time?"

That night after dinner, Kenny knew he needed to start telling his family what was going on. Casey came over as usual. Kenny's dad, Cody, and Ryan came downstairs to talk with Kenny about being late to the clinic.

"Kenny," started his dad, "Ryan was relying on you to be there to help out today. He has not needed you a lot lately, but he did today. You've had a lot time to do other things. This clinic was important to him and the skaters who signed up for it."

Rather than respond directly, Kenny took the stick out from behind the couch. "I have something to tell everyone. I think mom should hear it, too." They all walked upstairs, including Casey who was there to support Kenny.

Kenny told his mom, dad, and brothers what had happened. He told them about finding the stick in the cave, meeting the Storyteller in the casino, and the stories of the Flamethrowers.

His family did not know what to think of this story. Even with Casey there to back up the story, the family was not buying it.

Ryan spoke first. "So this is your excuse for being late? A flaming stick? Come on Kenny. A simple 'I overslept' would have been more believable!"

Next was mom's turn. "Kenny, this just sounds too wild and unreal. Do you really want us to believe you are now some Flamethrower leader?"

Kenny's dad jumped in, "Kenny I think you have had

too much time on your own this summer. You're going to be grounded the rest of the week, except for going to the rink to help Ryan. That's all you're doing the rest of the week."

Oh no thought Kenny, *I have to find that other stick. I can't do it if I'm grounded.*

Kenny started negotiating.

"Ryan, I am so sorry I was late today. I know it was important to you. But there is more to the story. The Storyteller told us there is an evil version of this stick. It must be found before anyone accidently finds it and touches it. If they do it will turn them evil."

"Geez, Kenny! Enough with the excuses!" said his dad with a great deal of annoyance. "You're not going any-where for the rest of the week. You need to calm down and get your head on straight. Remember what's impor-tant to this family. Ryan needs your help right now and you're going to help him. End of discussion." And with that his dad got up and left the room.

Kenny was very upset and stormed off to his room.

Casey was upset, too. Ryan tried to settle her down saying, "You're welcome to help out, Casey. I know you like to skate with us."

Casey turned towards Ryan and said loudly, "He's telling the truth! We need to find this stick! It's important! I plan to help him find the stick." And with that she turned and rushed out of the house.

Once home, Casey hopped online. She contacted Frank and Paul and told them what happened to Kenny. She needed their help to find the evil stick.

They made plans to meet in the morning at the cave and start looking. Casey posted a message for Kenny about their plans.

Kenny woke up early and Ryan took him to the rink. Ryan had two different clinics, and they would take all day. Kenny quickly checked online and saw that Casey had gotten Frank and Paul to go with her to the cave. He was glad they were going, but felt sad he wasn't.

Casey arrived with Frank and Paul at the cave entrance. She led the way while explaining where they had found the stick, where Ricky had fallen, and how there was an exit on top in case they got blocked in by Ron and his friends again. She told them about the stone box they were looking for and made it clear they were not to try and open the box and touch the stick, no matter what.

She led them to the room where they found the first stone box. It was still there, closed. Frank and Paul just stared in awe at the old stone box. They felt the cold hard surface and realized that Kenny had been telling at least some truth.

Frank said, "Dude, this is really real. Casey, you guys found that stick inside this stone tomb?"

Casey responded with a mix of relief and exasperation. "Yes! Just like we told you before, Kenny figured a way to fit his hand into the box, then grabbed the stick. While the stick bonded with him, the box opened for us."

Paul looked around the room, thinking about where to start looking for the twin stick.

"Casey, where do you think it is?" wondered Paul.

Frank jumped in, interrupting Casey. "Dude," he said proudly, "The Storyteller said it should be below or deeper than where the first stick would be found to ensure the good stick was found first."

Casey nodded in agreement and said, "The stone box should also look similar but darker and have some red markings on it. The red is a warning to not open the box."

Casey pointed to a small hole in the wall near the first box. "Let's move the box. I think I see a hole. We hadn't noticed that before."

Back at the rink Kenny was very distracted, trying to think of places he saw when they were looking for the rocks. He kept thinking about each room and passage they found. Was there an evil stone box in there?

Ryan was very frustrated with Kenny, because he wasn't helping out much and couldn't focus on anything. Ryan was yelling at Kenny to pay attention and move the pucks, set up the cones, and move the nets.

But Kenny could not help but think about his friends and what they might be finding right now.

...

Meanwhile, at the Brenton Mining Company, Briggs continued to look around where the kids had broken into the mine the night before.

Briggs went down many passages following the tennis shoe footprints. Unlike the workers who wore boots, the tennis shoes left prints that were very easy to follow. Briggs thought they might still be in the cave, or at least he could find out where they had spent their time. Briggs continued to follow the tracks to the opening of a small shaft. He was a very big man and size was now becoming an issue.

Briggs knelt down and started to crawl into the small shaft. He used his flashlight to look forward and see what was ahead. He saw there was a large opening up ahead and that he would be fine if he could just make it to the opening.

Briggs continued struggling on his hands and knees until he finally reached the opening. At last, he was able to stand up and stretch his large body, and look around.

And there it was. He saw what the kids had found in the wall and were trying to dig out. It looked like a large stone box that was pitch black in color and extremely cold to the touch.

He looked around and saw shovels, a pick ax, and other digging items. Briggs figured the kids had been interrupted because they dropped everything in place. They must have heard him coming and doubled back. *Maybe if I hurry I can catch them*, he thought.

But as he was about to turn around, he noticed a bit of carving in the wall, and it caught his attention. He looked more closely, holding the flashlight while running his other hand along the wall.

What he saw simply amazed him. It was very old, cold as ice, and very black in color. He could see something that looked like an owl yet had very distinct and harsh features.

Briggs decided to finish digging out the stone box.

He grabbed the pick ax and started swinging on each side of the stone box. He hit the stone box by accident, yet when he inspected it, he could see no chip or mark left behind. He was even more intrigued and resumed swinging the pick ax.

...

Back in the cave Casey, Frank, and Paul had no luck finding the stone box. They had looked everywhere they could see. *Buried lower than the first stick* kept ringing in Frank's head.

The three were growing frustrated. Casey walked over to Frank and said, "Let's take a break and go outside and call Ryan's cell. Let's see if we can talk with Kenny."

Frank and Paul were frustrated, too, and agreed they should take a break. Calling Kenny might help give them some ideas.

They reached the front of the cave. It was after noon now, and it had been a long day already. They called Ryan.

"Hello Ryan, is Kenny available?" she said nicely as she could, knowing Ryan was upset with her and Kenny.

"Sure," he said, "The players are in the locker room changing."

After a short wait, Casey heard Kenny's voice on the

phone.

"Hey, Kenny," said Casey.

"Any luck Casey? Did you find it?" Kenny started excitedly throwing questions at her.

"No," she interrupted, "And we have looked everywhere. I was calling to get some ideas from you."

He was disappointed for a second, then excited that he might still get to be a part of finding the evil stone box.

"I've been thinking. I was thinking about the shaft where Ricky fell. It's on a lower level and I never would have thought about going in there because of what happened to Ricky."

She thought about it for a second. "We didn't go in there either. I showed Frank and Paul the shaft where he fell, but you're right, we didn't think to go in there either."

She paused for a moment.

He could hear her nervous breathing. Finally he asked, "What's wrong?"

She slowly answered, "Okay, we'll go in there, but it's kind of creepy. That's where Ricky died. I'm not sure I like the idea of that."

He reassured her, "I know, but it will be okay, you

have Frank and Paul with you. Plus, it kind of makes sense, right? It has to be on a lower level and maybe they had found it before and that's why Ricky was in there. He found the stone box first."

Casey thought about that for a second, but it seemed too much. Ricky didn't die because he found some stone box. But she reluctantly agreed that they should check it out.

"Kenny says we need to check the shaft where Ricky died," she told Frank and Paul, who were watching her expectantly, impatient to hear what Kenny had to say.

A cold chill went down their backs and they squirmed.

Paul smiled nervously and did his best Bill Murray Ghostbusters impersonation, "I love this plan. I'm excited about this plan. We're gonna go in the same shaft where Ricky died and find an evil stick. Oh yeah, count me in."

Frank managed a small smile and Casey looked at Paul. "You don't have to go, Paul, if you don't want to," she snapped.

"No way are you going to find that crazy evil stick without me!" he answered back.

...

Briggs was getting tired but he was determined. He continued to pick at the cave wall to unearth the stone box. He was getting close. He could see the weight of the heavy box starting to shift downward. He knew it would be freed soon. He kept swinging away.

...

Casey made it to the shaft where Ricky had died and pointed her flashlight down into the darkness. It was a good drop and they needed rope. Frank agreed to stay on top in case anything happened, so he could go get help. Paul and Casey were lowered down into the shaft and when they arrived at the bottom they could see a lot of passages.

Frank called down, "What do you see?"

Casey yelled back up, "There are a lot of tunnels down here. Any ideas?"

Frank thought for just a moment, "Yes, start going in the direction under where we found the stick. Look at me."

Paul and Casey looked up. Frank pointed to the room where the first stick was found and said, "Go this direction and start there. If the Storyteller was right you want to go that direction."

Casey and Paul nodded and started down the tunnel.

Paul hesitated, and then said, "Got crumbs?"

Casey smiled. Then she put an "X" on the wall so they'd know they had taken that tunnel.

...

Briggs stopped digging for a moment. *What was that sound? Are those voices? The kids must be coming back.*

Briggs decided to keep digging, but faster. *Let them find me. They are going to be more scared of me then worrying about some box.*

He realized the box was mostly free, and he grabbed an end of the stone box and pulled it free from the wall. It crashed to the ground with a deafening sound which seemed all the louder in the small chamber.

He saw a large red X on the top and some other characters in red. *Looks like a warning message of some type* he thought. *There must be something very special inside.*

...

Casey stopped after hearing a loud crashing sound. "Paul, did you hear that?" she asked.

"Yeah," said Paul, "Sounded close."

Casey and Paul pointed the flashlights all around, but couldn't see anything or anyone. And now all they could hear was their own breathing.

Little did they know that directly beneath them, Briggs was opening the evil stone box.

Suddenly another loud sound came from somewhere in the tunnels. This time, though, they could tell it was a person. A person screaming.

Casey and Paul started running back to where Frank was. While she was running, Casey thought back to the last time she'd heard a scream like that. She knew someone must have opened the evil stone box and was bonding to the stick, just like Kenny had.

"Frank! Pull us up now! Hurry! We're too late. Someone else found the evil stick! Hurry!"

Frank pulled the rope, bringing up first Casey then Paul. The three of them then ran as hard as they could.

When they reached the cave entrance, Paul asked, "How do you know that someone found the evil stone box?"

Casey said, "Because Kenny made that same sound when he reached in and grabbed the stick. Someone found it. Someone has the evil stick."

Frank looked at Casey, "Then where are they?"

Casey shook her head, "In there, for now."

...

Briggs was feeling the same pain Kenny had. And the stone box had opened the same way it had for Kenny. Briggs had been able to remove the stick.

He stared at the shape of the stick, the dark black handle and an owl for a head. He was awed by the detail. It gave him a feeling of horror. It was an owl, he knew, but somehow a very angry-looking owl.

As Briggs continued to inspect the stick, he felt the pain continue up his arms, shoulders, and eventually his head. He tried to drop the stick but could not.

Panic set in and he felt like his head was exploding. He wanted to hold his head, to press on it with his large hands. But his hands seemed glued to the stick. He could not do anything to stop the incredible pain in his head.

Soon the big body of Briggs fell down to the ground; he'd passed out.

16

Breakout

Briggs awoke confused and disoriented. He remembered finding something - a stone box - which had a stick in it. Now the stick was in his hands.

Briggs got to his feet and suddenly felt a wave of anger come over him. These kids had driven him deep into the mine. He was angry at everyone who thought he had killed Ricky and sent him to prison. His anger was consuming his thoughts and he let out a deep, primal yell, "AAARRRRGGGHHH!"

Cody Conley was sitting in his office. He got up as he heard guys scrambling outside.

"Boss! Boss! Someone in the mine is going crazy! He's throwing stuff around, acting crazy," said one of the workers.

Cody asked, "Who is it? Do you know?"

"No, no one wants to get close enough to see who it is," he said, trying to catch his breath.

Cody asked, "Do you know where Dan is?"

The worker nodded. "Dan's by the truck, right over there," pointing towards the large dump truck.

Cody told someone to tell Dan to meet him at the entrance to the mine.

"We're going to need to go in and take a look," he added.

But just then Briggs came out of the mine, running at full speed with his new-found stick.

Cody could see Briggs's eyes were wide open and his face had a crazy look. Briggs was swinging the stick and smashing everything in his way. He hit boxes, tables, sheds, anything within swinging distance. Cody knew Briggs, but he had never seen him like this. Cody was nervous and began to worry for his guys. Briggs was a beast of a man. One person was not going to slow him down, let alone stop him.

Briggs raced to the parking lot and started smashing truck windows and doors, just hammering them with the stick. Briggs stopped and screamed again. Then he looked down at the stick in his hands. To those watching, it almost seemed like he was listening to the stick.

Briggs reached the end of the parking lot, then turned and ran down the road. No one followed him. Cody checked around to see who was injured. Dan looked pretty scared when he reached him.

"Dan, you okay?" asked Cody.

"A little shaken up, Cody. Was that Briggs doing that?" asked Dan.

"Yeah, but I've never seen him act that way before," answered Cody.

Dan asked the obvious questions, "What are we going to do? Where is he going?"

Cody thought for a second, *Dan has a point, where is he going?*

Cody remembered what Kenny had said. Briggs did have something that looked like the stick that Kenny showed them last night. He wasn't sure what to believe, but he knew he should let Kenny know what was going on. Maybe there was something to his wild story.

Cody turned back to Dan, "I've got an idea. I've gotta get Kenny. Can you help everyone get fixed up here?"

Dan told him, "Sure, no worries, go."

Cody jumped into his truck and took off.

Casey, Frank, and Paul sat outside the cave, depressed and defeated, knowing they had to tell Kenny they'd failed and someone else had found the stick.

Paul asked, "Who do you think found the stick? Do you think it was that Ron kid?"

Casey thought for a few moments. "I don't know, but we should head out, find Kenny, and figure out what we're going to do. We never talked about what would happen if someone else found the evil stick. We were supposed to stop that from happening."

Frank heard something, turned, and saw Briggs.

Frank pointed, "Look! Someone's coming!"

Just as Casey and Paul turned around, Briggs was right there, running straight at them. He was not slowing down. They all could see the crazy look in his eyes. He did not even seem to notice them.

Casey called out, "Look he has the stick! He has the evil –"

Just as she tried to finish her sentence, Briggs ran his

shoulder right into her chest and sent her flying into the air.

Frank and Paul both rushed to help her, while Briggs continued at full speed into the cave.

"Casey! You alright?" asked Frank in shock.

Casey was stunned and slowly moved her right hand towards her face.

"Wow...he hit me harder than either of you two ever have," she said as she spit some blood out of her mouth.

Paul held up his hand, "Hold on Casey, take it easy. You just got your bell rung pretty good."

Casey hesitated, then slowly sat up. "We need to get back and talk with Kenny. He should be done with clinics by now. Let's get over there." Casey slowly but determinedly got up, while Paul and Frank tried to help. She shooed them off.

Casey, Frank, and Paul pulled into Kenny's driveway right as Ryan and Kenny arrived. Kenny got out of the car, looking at them to see if they had any good news.

"So?" asked Kenny expectantly.

Frank answered, "Sorry, dude."

"What happened?" Kenny asked.

"Somebody else found it first," said Casey.

Kenny noticed the blood on the corner of Casey's mouth. He asked her, "What happened? Are you hurt?"

Casey said, "We went down the shaft where Ricky died and we could hear someone opening the stone box. But we never saw them. They must have been in another shaft right below us."

Kenny was disappointed, but also knew from looking at his friends covered in dirt and mud they had been working hard all day to find the stick.

"It's okay," Kenny said supportively. "Did you see who found it? And how did you get hurt?"

Paul answered, "Some really big dude came running at us carrying the evil stick. He face-planted Casey and ran inside the cave."

Kenny wondered, *did he know the rocks were in the cave? How would he know?*

Kenny continued, "Casey, did he find the rocks?"

She answered, "I don't know. We didn't hang around to see. We had to come here to figure out what to do."

As they were standing in the front yard talking, Kenny's dad, Cody, pulled up in his truck. He stopped and jumped out his truck, moving quickly towards the group now assembled in the front yard.

Cody called to Kenny, "I think we found that stick.

Briggs came running out of the mine, out of control and destroying things. He was carrying a black stick like the one you found."

Kenny was stunned. His Dad was starting to believe! Kenny started thinking, *Briggs...of all people to find the stick, and it had to be the biggest guy we know! What should we do next? The evil stick was now out of the stone box. Briggs' size, along with the evil stick...plus he was in the cave with the red rocks.* Kenny's head was spinning.

"We have to stop him!" Kenny blurted out, "We have to get the evil stick back!"

Frank looked at him, "Dude, that's one big guy."

Casey was quietly listening, but she knew she had to speak. "Kenny, you have the power of the Flamethrower. You need to be the one to face him. You can use your powers to hurt him, and get the stick away from him."

Frank, Paul, Ryan, and Cody all looked at each other and stared thinking the same thing: *Kenny?*

Kenny looked at Casey and asked, "Do you remember if the Storyteller said what we had to do if someone got the stick?"

Casey thought for a moment and answered, "No. He didn't say anything specific, except that the evil in the stick would take over the person who possessed it. Turn them evil."

Paul asked, "Why would it turn someone evil?"

Casey responded, "The good stick has free will, choice as its power, the evil stick is the opposite. It takes away choice and forces him against his will."

Kenny nodded, "We need to find him and stop him. You said he's in the cave. Let's start there."

Each of them stood still, looking at Kenny. He'd never shown this much passion and resolve about anything before. *Never!*

Cody could tell Kenny was serious, and he knew they needed to track down Briggs. So he backed his son, saying, "Alright let's go get him. Come on!"

Kenny smiled and started moving quickly towards the trucks.

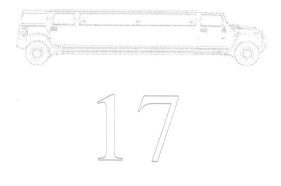

17

Briggs' Revenge

Kenny and the gang drove up to the cave to confront Briggs. When they arrived, Kenny's first question was answered. Briggs had indeed found the red rocks and was practicing throwing the fireballs down the hill, hitting rocks and trees and causing destruction.

When they got out of the trucks, Briggs noticed them and started aiming his fireballs at them. Soon they were under attack and they ran, scrambling for cover. Briggs definitely had the advantage, being up on the hill.

Casey looked up the hill and saw that Briggs had a pack of red rocks near his feet.

She leaned over to the guys and said, "Hey, we need to get the red rocks from him."

Kenny nodded frantically in agreement. "We need to get him away from the cave, too. He has an unlimited supply of red rocks in there!"

The group started throwing out ideas for luring Briggs away from the cave.

Meanwhile, Briggs continued to throw fireballs down towards the trucks. None were hitting their mark, but he seemed to be improving his aim with each throw.

Frank had an idea, "Kenny, you need to stand up to Briggs and show him we have a Flamethrower stick, too. Show him we have the same ability to throw fireballs!"

Frank continued, "I can sneak up and grab his ammo. He'll need to decide whether to follow me and get his ammo back, or face Kenny without any red rocks. Kenny, you have to prevent him from getting more ammo in the cave. If you block the cave he will have to follow us."

Paul nodded at Frank but wondered, "Okay, but where are you going after you get the red rocks?"

"Dude, I don't have the whole plan, okay? We just gotta figure out the rest," answered Frank, flustered but ready to act.

"Frank," said Casey. "After you grab the pack, get

back to Cody's truck and we'll drive away. He won't be able to keep up. Kenny, you keep guard to prevent him from getting back into the cave."

"Wait, where are we going to drive to?" asked Paul.

"It doesn't matter," said Casey.

Then she turned to Ryan, "Can you go to the casino and get the Storyteller? Let him know what happened and ask him to come help us."

Kenny reinforced Casey's idea. "Yes, we need the Storyteller to help us stop Briggs! If we can get the ammo away from him, we can limit the damage he can do for awhile."

Ryan nodded and asked, "What should I tell him?"

Kenny answered, "Tell him you're my brother and we need help, that the wrong person found the evil stick."

With that Ryan moved back to his truck and took off. Briggs threw a couple of shots his direction, trying to stop him, but missed.

Kenny grabbed his backpack and looked up.

"Frank, I'll give you five minutes to get in place, then I'll start firing to create a distraction."

Frank nodded and started jogging up the left side of the hill. Briggs now seemed focused on Cody's truck and kept firing at it as he perfected his throwing skills.

Kenny hiked up the right side of the hill. He found a good flat spot to dump out the red rocks in his backpack, and with room to stand and throw directly at Briggs. After unloading the backpack, Kenny stood up and stared directly at Briggs.

Briggs saw him now, and his attention became focused completely on Kenny. He watched as Kenny lifted his Flamethrower stick high in the air. Briggs eyes widened and he realized that Kenny had what looked like a matching stick. Briggs reached down and put a red rock in the evil stick and threw a shot towards Kenny.

Kenny dodged the shot and then loaded his own red rock. Kenny stood tall to make sure Briggs could see his red rock on fire. Kenny stood there, feeling the power of the stick. His confidence was growing in what he could do with it.

Kenny stepped forward and threw his first shot. The shot flew hard and fast. The rock was bright orange on fire and went straight at Briggs head.

Briggs, seeing the fireball coming, ducked and swung the evil stick to deflect it. He seemed to pause, trying to figure out how Kenny had the same weapon he did.

Kenny threw another shot, then another. Briggs didn't respond at first. But then he started to run straight towards Kenny.

Kenny, seeing Briggs charging him, yelled out, "Now!"

Then Kenny started running away from Briggs.

As Briggs continued running towards Kenny, Frank raced towards the abandoned red rocks. Briggs had only run a few yards towards Kenny when he realized that someone was behind him.

Kenny noticed that Briggs was hesitating, so he threw a few more fireballs as he ran. But Briggs had stopped, clearly trying to figure out what was going on. He needed his red rocks, and yet he wanted to defeat Kenny, his biggest threat. He knew he couldn't go in two directions at once, but he wasn't sure which was more important. His hesitation gave Frank the break he needed.

As the others loudly cheered him on, Frank grabbed Briggs's pack of red rocks and took off running back down the hill.

Briggs turned and started chasing Frank down the hill. Kenny knew he had not gotten Briggs far enough away from him, and needed to recapture the big man's attention.

Kenny grabbed a rock, took his time, and threw a strong shot right at Briggs. The shot hit Briggs right in

the shoulder, and down he went. Briggs tumbled rough-
ly down the hill allowing Frank to get safely to the truck.

Briggs shook off the hit and looked back up the hill
at Kenny. Kenny stood tall, knowing he now had the
high ground.

Briggs growled furiously towards Kenny. But Kenny
felt strong now. He could hurt Briggs and they both
knew it.

Frank reached the truck and they started driving
away. Frank felt ecstatic, thinking they'd gotten away
easy. But when he looked back, Briggs was running after
them, and surprisingly gaining ground.

Briggs was discovering something as he ran. He was
feeling the urge to jump. When he jumped, he covered
a great distance. He didn't understand how, but he
could jump over things. Big things like cars and trees.

When Frank looked back again, he saw Briggs almost
flying towards them.

Frank yelled out, "Dude, we're gonna need to go faster. A LOT faster!"

Seeing the look of fear on Frank's face, Cody, who
was driving, suddenly felt a bit of panic.

"Frank, no one can run this fast. We're going 40 miles
per hour!" exclaimed Cody.

Frank anxiously looked back again. "He's kinda jumping... and flying...right behind us. I swear it!"

Kenny ran down from the hill and watched as Briggs was running after the truck. He thought, *okay our plan has worked so far.*

Casey, who had stayed near the cave, started running towards Kenny. Just as she reached him, a long white stretch limo was pulling up behind her.

White Crane called out, "We need to catch that truck and the guy who is chasing them." He motioned to Kenny and Casey to get into the limousine.

But Kenny argued, "I have to stay here and protect the cave and the red rocks. Briggs can't be allowed to come back and reload!"

Kenny paused then insisted, "It's my job to protect the cave."

White Crane put up his hands as if to calm Kenny, and prepare him to hear what he has to say. "Kenny, we need to save your family. They're trapped in that truck. He will catch them."

"How can he catch the truck?" questioned Kenny.

"Trust me Kenny, we need to go."

Casey turned to Kenny, "You wanted Ryan to get White Crane. You must have wanted him for a reason.

You should listen to him."

Kenny reluctantly gave in, and followed Casey into the limousine. The inside of the limousine was white, just like the office at the casino. White carpet, white seats, white lights, and even white buttons for everything.

"You sure like your white," teased Casey.

"I am well respected by my Nation. They treat me well and these are some of the comforts they have given me."

Casey questioned, "But why white?"

He answered, chuckling, "My name is White Crane. Is that really such a stretch for your young mind?"

Casey felt her cheeks flush in embarrassment; she hadn't seen the obvious!

Kenny looked out the window and saw kids playing roller hockey in the tennis courts. He recognized the kids from the clinics he had taught earlier in the day. They were young and dressed in their favorite players uniforms. The kids seem unaware of what was going on.

The smallest kid was the fastest, wearing a jersey that went below his knees. Kenny watched the kid weave in and out of his friends, scoring a goal and celebrating with a huge smile on his face.

White Crane looked at Kenny and his face seemed to

go stone cold. "Kenny, the evil stick has gained power over a person of great physical size."

Kenny nodded and reinforced White Crane's feeling. "Briggs works for my dad as a security guard. He is a really big, scary guy. He was accused and sent to prison for killing a kid named Ricky. My dad said he didn't do it."

Kenny watched the face of White Crane for clues to what he would say next. But White Crane only stared back. Kenny knew something scary was going to come next and he began to shiver.

White Crane finally spoke, "Do you remember I told you that the Flamethrower stick bonds to its owner? And will only work for that warrior while they are alive?"

Kenny nodded that he remembered. But he didn't like where this was going.

White Crane continued, "The same is true for the evil stick. Briggs has now bonded with the stick and his powers will continue until he is dead."

Casey turned to Kenny as if she understood. Kenny looked at her, not quite following what White Crane meant. He knew the stick only had powers for him and when he died they would be passed on to another.

Casey leaned forward, "If I understand, we have to kill

Briggs to stop him."

Kenny tried to stand up but hit his head on the roof and *WHAM* landed back in his seat. His head hurt and his heart was pounding. He was feeling faint and frantic.

"NO WAY!" he shouted. "I'm not going to kill anyone!"

White Crane held out his hands again to calm Kenny down. "Kenny, once a stick has bonded to a person, that person has the powers until they die. According to our legends the person who has bonded with the evil stick must die to end the destruction."

"What destruction? He hasn't really done anything yet. And we took away his ammunition. He has less power without the red rocks. Maybe we can..."

Kenny's voice trailed off as Casey pointed outside the window and Kenny saw Briggs leaping high into the air and gaining on his dad's truck.

Kenny lowered his tone to ask, in shock, "How can he do that? Jump like that?"

White Crane answered, "The owner of the stick inherits many of the same powers of the animal the stick represents. Briggs is learning that he has the power to fly."

Kenny and Casey stared out the window as they

183

watched Briggs get closer and closer to the fleeing truck. They could see the truck was speeding up, but Briggs was gaining.

"We have to save them. He wants those red rocks back. He's gonna hurt them," said Kenny.

White Crane nodded, "The evil stick seems to have chosen someone who is full of rage and anger. He wants revenge on the community. He will not stop. The evil stick has blinded him and given him the power to carry out his revenge."

Kenny's heart was pounding. He could barely hear himself think. His whole head was pounding from all the issues that now confronted him. His family and friends were in real danger. Briggs was about to recapture his weapons of destruction, and then would destroy his hometown. *And the only way to stop Briggs was to kill him? Why was this happening?*

Kenny started to lash out at White Crane, "Why me? Why do I have to do this? Why not someone else? What if I fail?"

Casey could see Kenny was freaking out. Her mind was racing, trying to figure out a solution. *What could they do? They had to stop Briggs. They had to save Kenny's dad, their friends, and the town.* Casey stared at

Kenny. She was hoping for an idea.

Kenny took a breath. He remembered his dad teaching him that when the game is getting crazy, slow your breathing and slow the game down in your head. Don't just react; slow down and see the situation. Then find a solution, see the answer, or find a way.

Kenny took another slow breath. This time he calmed his mind down. He laid out the options before him. He needed to get the power away from Briggs. They had taken one item from him, but not the other.

He started to explain it out loud, "We need to get the stick away from him. His source of power comes from the stick, too. Not just the red rocks."

Casey nodded, "Yes, we didn't think to take the stick from him, too. We were only worried about the red rocks."

She was feeling a little shook up that she'd missed this rather obvious solution, too. She'd always felt herself the logical one. But it was Kenny who was thinking this through. She was also rather impressed!

White Crane sat back as if he knew where Kenny was going with this. "You have an interesting idea there, don't you? You are wondering if we can get the evil stick away from Briggs, would his powers be reduced or stopped."

Kenny looked calmly at White Crane, "Exactly. What if we could return the evil stick to the stone box without killing him? Would the powers stop because the stick is trapped inside the box again?"

White Crane tried to remember all the stories he had been told about the Flamethrowers and their powers. He remembered how the evil sticks had been stopped in the past. But there were only stories of death for the evil stick holder.

"Kenny, until now the person who possessed the evil stick was killed to end the destruction. I do not know if what you are asking will work. I cannot say one way or the other."

Kenny leaned forward, feeling confident and in command. "We need to try and save Briggs from the evil stick, too. He has been through too much to die this way. We owe it to him to try."

White Crane leaned forward to challenge Kenny. "What you're trying to do is very dangerous. He will not recognize you, or show you any mercy. He simply wants to destroy things. You are risking your life, your family, and your town."

"Kenny is right, we have to try!" Casey said emphatically. "If it doesn't work we can do it your way. But we have to try and save him from the evil in the stick."

White Crane from saw the passion in their eyes that they wanted to do this. He realized maybe this was why Kenny received the Flamethrower power. His compassion.

White Crane spoke, "Very well. We will need someone to go and get the evil stone box and bring it to town. The quicker we can get the stick back into the stone box the safer we will all be. If it fails, we will know very quickly. And you will know what you need to do then."

Kenny and Casey nodded in agreement.

But Kenny could not imagine having to kill.

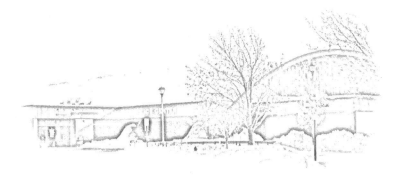

Casey Falls

Frank looked out the back of the truck. Briggs was still gaining on them.

"Dude, he's catching up!" yelled Frank. "We better get out on the highway and open it up."

"Too late, guys, we can't get to the highway," said Cody. "We're headed into town and I can't go any faster without hurting someone."

"Can't we turn around?" asked Paul.

"No!" said Frank, "He is right on our ass. He's going to pounce on us if we don't get out of here."

Frank looked back and saw Briggs high in the air coming in, right on top of them.

"Turn!" yelled Frank.

Cody turned left quickly and Briggs landed right next to the truck. Briggs swung the evil stick and slammed it into the back right-end of the truck, making a crashing sound.

Cody looked back. "Boys, you okay? Where is he?"

"We're fine! Don't stop!" screamed Frank.

Cody found himself driving right towards the ice arena parking lot.

Cody said, "I have an idea, guys."

Cody drove full speed into the empty parking lot. Cody went wide, trying to turn around and head back out. *Okay, now I can lead him out to the highway* he thought, hopefully.

Frank and Paul were hanging on as Cody turned sharper to make the final corner out of the parking lot. Cody could see the exit and started to feel like his plan was going to work.

Inside the limousine, the driver was closing in behind the truck. They were all focused on Briggs, watching him

189

gaining on the truck.

The driver called back to White Crane, "You need to see this! The big guy is catching the truck. You better be ready!"

Briggs was now fifty feet in the air, crashing down near the truck. Cody had turned the truck just in time to avoid Briggs, who would have landed in the back of the truck.

White Crane called out to the driver, "You need to get us there now!"

The driver pushed his foot to the floor and the limousine picked up speed, heading towards the ice arena. The truck was still in the parking lot but was now headed towards the street.

White Crane called out, "Stop right here! We're getting out! Hurry!"

He could see Cody was trying to turn around in the parking lot but wasn't going to make it.

"Kenny load up and let's go!" said White Crane.

Kenny jumped into action and grabbed his Flamethrower stick and backpack. He bolted out of the limousine door, looking up just as Briggs made one more jump towards the truck that was now trying to speed out of the parking lot.

Casey stepped out of the limousine and saw Briggs coming down on top of the truck.

She yelled, "Kenny! You have to stop him!"

Kenny reached in and grabbed a red rock, and loaded it. He sent a shot flying towards Briggs, but realized it was too late.

BAM! Briggs had landed in the back of the truck, sending it out of control. The truck swerved as Cody tried to control it. He slammed on the brakes, sending Briggs flying over the cab of the truck.

Kenny loaded his next fireball. As Briggs recovered from his fall, Kenny threw a shot that slammed into the ground right near Briggs' left leg. Briggs fell to the ground, stunned. As he got up again, he saw Kenny standing there, ready with another shot. He let out a howling scream and began running towards Kenny.

Kenny held steady and took a breath. He threw his next shot and hit Briggs in the right knee, sending him to the ground in pain.

Kenny was feeling confident. His aim was good, and Briggs was without ammunition and on the ground.

Briggs realized he was definitely at a disadvantage. Looking around, he saw the ice arena. He needed somewhere to hide, so he ran, limping, flailing his arms, into the ice arena.

With Briggs out of the equation for now, Casey ran towards the truck to see if Frank and Paul were okay. "Frank, Paul!" she called out.

Frank was climbing out of the back door of the truck. "We're okay," he reassured her, "A little wonky though. Where's Briggs?"

Kenny had reached them now. "He's in the rink. I think he's a bit shook up. I nailed him in the knee."

"Good," said Paul, getting out now, "Let's finish this."

"Hold on," said Casey, "We need a plan."

Kenny said, "We can't go in there. He has the advantage, with benches and machines he can throw and block me. Plus, we will destroy the arena trying to get him. We can't let that happen. We need to draw him out."

Frank replied, "Dude, how are we going to draw him out? Why would he leave the rink?"

Casey answered, "We still have his red rocks, right?"

Paul looked at the pack in Cody's truck, "Yeah, we got 'em. I'll go get 'em."

Paul jogged over to the truck and grabbed the pack.

Casey looked over at Kenny, "We need that stone box."

With all the excitement, Kenny had forgotten that they still needed the evil stone box. They needed it so they could immediately put the evil stick back in. Then they could see if Briggs would recover, or still needed to be destroyed.

Kenny turned to Frank, "We need a huge favor, Frank."

"Dude," was Frank's only response.

Casey started to explain in very fast words. "Guys, we need the evil stone box where Briggs found the evil stick. We think if we can take the stick from him and put it back in the stone box, it will lose its power and stop controlling Briggs."

Paul looked at Casey, then Kenny. "Where is it?"

Casey reminded him, "Remember, he found it right below us in the shaft? We heard him when he opened it."

Cody told them, "Briggs came out of the shaft in the mine area. I think it was near where the teens were breaking in. I think I know where to look."

Kenny reminded them, "The stone box is very heavy. We couldn't carry it."

His dad said, "We have just the thing for that. We'll go back and get the box and meet you back here."

Kenny turned and looked for the Storyteller, but the limousine was gone. *Where did he go?*

Kenny and Casey watched as Cody, Frank, and Paul got into the truck. Kenny looked at the truck as it drove away. The back end had a large smashed-in area where Briggs had landed. The rear wheels also looked a bit bent, but it seemed to be okay as they drove away.

Kenny turned back to see that Casey had picked up Briggs' pack of red rocks. Casey was about fifty feet away from Kenny and she called back to him, "We need to get this to a safe spot and keep him trapped inside until they get back. Then we can –"

Casey stopped talking as she saw Kenny's face go whiter than normal. Kenny was yelling something but Casey couldn't hear it. She turned and saw Briggs running right at her.

Kenny ran at Briggs as if to challenge him, but Briggs could see Kenny had no red rocks so he turned his attention on Casey.

Casey turned to run away from Briggs. She thought maybe she could throw the pack, but it was so full and heavy that she couldn't do anything with it.

She tried to run, but Briggs had already left the ground and had leapt into the air. Kenny tried desperately to get between her and Briggs. But Briggs landed right next to her, and the force crashed Casey into the ground.

Casey went head-first into the asphalt parking lot and the pack fell from her hands. Briggs grabbed the pack and threw it over his shoulder. As Kenny approached, Briggs swung the evil stick, hitting Kenny in the chest and knocking him to the ground. Everything went black.

Kenny was unconscious, crumpled on the ground near Casey. As he lay there, he saw a bright light. He tried to focus his eyes as someone approached him. It was a man with long black hair and a strong body. He carried the owl stick in his right hand. Kenny watched as the man stood over him. Kenny could not move.

"Kenny," said the man, "I am Ryukyu of the Owl Nation. I was the first Flamethrower of my Nation. My stick has now been passed to you. You are a Flamethrower and must now save your village from the evil that has been awakened."

Kenny was trying to understand what was going on. *Was this real? Was his mind playing tricks on him?*

Kenny asked in confusion, "How can I defeat the evil?"

Ryukyu replied, "The person who carries the evil stick

can only be destroyed by a shot from your stick, through his heart."

It was the same answer as the Storyteller. But Kenny still wanted to save Briggs. "Can we defeat the evil stick without killing the person carrying the stick?"

Ryukyu bent down and looked into Kenny's eyes. Kenny was nervous but not frightened.

Ryukyu then spoke, "Kenny, you are a compassionate warrior. You do not want to kill this person who is threatening your village and hurt your friend."

He paused, looking at Kenny's eyes. "The answer is yes, you can stop him without killing him. But you must remove the stick from his possession and return it immediately to its resting spot. Only then will the evil be contained again."

I knew it! thought Kenny triumphantly.

He asked another question, "Why was I chosen for this?"

Ryukyu thought carefully, "The Flamethrower stick is not always passed down from father to son. You have a destiny with the stick that will be revealed. For now, your focus is to stop the evil that is threatening your village. Return the evil stick to its stone box."

Ryukyu leaned forward and continued, "Listen to the

owl stick. Its powers can bc yours, but you must close your eyes and let it guide you and teach you. The stick has had many owners before you that have learned its ways. Trust in yourself. Let the Flamethrower stick be your mentor."

With those words, Ryukyu turned and walked away from Kenny. The light grew dimmer as Ryukyu moved away, and suddenly it was dark again.

Kenny awoke, hearing someone calling his name. "Kenny! Kenny! Kenny, you alright?" Kenny recognized the voice now, it was his mom. He started to get up but he felt a huge weight on his chest.

"Oh man, what happened?" asked Kenny, very disoriented.

"Your father called and told me to come down to the arena. When I got here you and Casey were both on the ground," said his mom.

Kenny remembered. Casey had been hit by Briggs. He slowly got up through the pain and looked for Casey. She was still lying on the ground.

"Casey!" he cried out.

"Careful Kenny," said his mom.

"I think she's hurt pretty bad. I called 911. They're on the way."

Kenny looked down at Casey. Her arm was badly bruised, her face badly scratched where she hit the pavement, and her left leg was bent back. He could see her breathing was shallow. He sat there beside her, numb.

He thought about all the times they had skated together, and he began to tear up. She believed in him, in this wild story of Flamethrowers and red rocks. He felt responsible for getting her hurt. He wasn't sure what he should do next.

Kenny's mom grabbed his hand and put her arm around him. They heard the first siren as it approached, and Kenny looked up, wiping his eyes.

Just as the police car came around the corner, BAM! Kenny saw a fireball hit the police car. He had forgotten Briggs was loose and armed.

Kenny jumped to his feet and looked around for his stick and backpack. He saw them and then glanced back at Casey. His resolve returned and he knew he had to stop Briggs.

"Mom, I have to stop him. He has to be stopped."

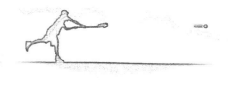

19

A Flamethrower Emerges

Kenny picked up the Flamethrower stick and threw his backpack on. He ran towards the police car. The police officer was fine and Kenny pointed him back to Casey and his mom.

Kenny could see that the officer was asking questions, but nothing registered in his head. It was like a distant sound; instead Kenny was focused on finding Briggs. It was his job, he thought, *my job to stop Briggs.*

He crossed the intersection. Traffic had stopped. He looked around, trying to locate Briggs.

Kenny started to worry about what he had to do.

What if they didn't find the evil stone box?

Would I have to kill Briggs?

Would the stone box even work?

Was Casey going to be okay?

His mind was racing with questions for which he had no answers.

Kenny could hear the ambulance approaching. *I need to find him before he attacks them, too. Where is he?*

He wondered how Briggs had known where to find the cave with the red rocks. Did the stick tell Briggs where to look?

Could his stick be talking to him and he wasn't listening? Ryukyu had told him the stick had powers he had not used yet. He closed his eyes and tried to clear his mind.

He put both hands on the Flamethrower stick. He then focused his thoughts, *Where is Briggs?* The head of the Flamethrower stick started to pull to the left. Kenny turned to his left. The pulling stopped. Kenny opened his eyes. He was facing a street but saw nothing but parked cars. Kenny, trusting the stick, started moving straight ahead and placed a red rock in the pocket of the Flamethrower stick.

As the ambulance came into the intersection, Kenny

kept his focus forward, watching for Briggs. Just as Kenny expected, Briggs made his move. He was directly in front of Kenny, about 100 yards away. Briggs was focused on the ambulance and did not appear to see Kenny.

Kenny saw his chance and threw the fireball right at Briggs.

BAM! The fireball slammed into the building just inches from Briggs' head, making him fall backwards. He looked up, surprised Kenny had found him.

Kenny had protected the ambulance. Kenny grabbed another red rock and started running while cradling it in the stick. Briggs was hurt, and he moved slowly behind the building and lumbered down the street.

Kenny followed Briggs around the building. He was feeling great about having Briggs on the run. Kenny turned the corner and he could see Briggs slowly moving at the end of the street. Kenny launched another shot. It landed at Briggs' feet, sending him to the ground as it exploded.

Kenny, excited from knocking Briggs down, started running towards the big wounded man. Kenny was hoping that Briggs had dropped his stick. But he knew it would not be that easy.

201

Kenny needed to find a way to get the evil stick away from Briggs. Even though Briggs had hurt Casey, he still didn't want to kill him. He believed his dad. He believed that Briggs had been innocent of killing Ricky.

Kenny followed Briggs around the next building. This time, Briggs was standing out in the open, ready to throw back at Kenny.

A surprised Kenny ducked right as Briggs unleashed a hard shot. The rock flew past Kenny and hit a car behind him. The fireball blew the car apart and sent Kenny face-first into the ground.

Kenny scrambled to his feet and started running away from Briggs. *He's got me on the run now,* he thought.

Kenny was scared, remembering how Briggs had chased the truck earlier. Running, jumping, he had caught them fast.

He made his turns quick and often, to try to confuse Briggs. Kenny zigzagged around buildings and cars, in downtown Brenton.

He could hear Briggs' loud steps and jumps around him but couldn't quite figure out what direction the sounds were coming from. Briggs could not get very close because Kenny was constantly changing directions.

Kenny then tried jumping like he had seen Briggs do

earlier. But he did not get very far at first. But after a few jumps he was getting higher off the ground.

But with the running and jumping Kenny was getting tired, and he knew he was not going to last much longer. He needed to find another way to slow down Briggs. Kenny looked ahead and saw a small opening between two brick buildings.

Kenny decided it would be a good place to take a stand. He loaded a red rock into the stick and ran between the brick buildings.

Kenny turned, and as Briggs tried to follow him down the alley, Kenny took his shot. The rock missed Briggs did but managed to stop him.

As Briggs stood there letting the dust settle, he decided to start firing back. He lobbed shot after shot at Kenny, hitting the brick walls around Kenny. The shots exploded against the brick wall, sending pieces flying everywhere. Kenny could feel the pieces of brick raining on him, though he was not feeling any pain.

While the dust cloud swirled, Kenny knew it was a good time to move. He ran behind a car and watched as Briggs walked out of the dust cloud. Kenny saw a chance to shoot, but Briggs saw him first and quickly took his shot at Kenny. He hit the car, sending a fireball into the air.

Kenny had been thrown back from the blast. He went to reload, but realized he had dropped his Flamethrower stick. Kenny frantically looked for the stick, but he couldn't see it anywhere. He was feeling overwhelmed by the chaos and knew he was vulnerable. He wanted to slowly survey the scene, calmly, like he'd been taught. But the situation wasn't going to allow that.

Briggs quickly realized that Kenny didn't have his stick. Briggs started walking slowly towards Kenny. He placed a red rock into the pocket of the black evil stick, and paused to allow it to build into a full fireball.

Kenny could now see the evil stick up close. The stick was solid black, with pointed bones twisting around the top and handle.

Kenny sat frozen in place, thinking how all this started. *What are these powers? How did all this happen so quickly? Why am I staring at the security guard who works for my dad and who was about to kill me?*

Briggs pulled the black evil stick back in preparation for the throw. Just as he was about to throw forward, Briggs became distracted by the sudden screeching of tires.

Kenny's eyes followed the sound and saw his dad's

truck pull up. *They're back!*

Kenny took advantage of Briggs' distraction and did another fast scan of the area. He saw the stick, under a car!

Briggs had turned his attention towards Cody's truck. The evil stick was loaded with a full-power red rock. He threw it directly at the truck.

Cody saw the fireball arching towards him and turned sharply. The fireball just missed the backside of the truck. But the impromptu turn had caused Cody to lose control of the truck and he slammed into the back of a parked car.

Kenny scrambled to his feet. He ran towards the Flamethrower stick under the car, reached and grabbed the stick. He looked up just in time to see Briggs approaching the truck. Kenny thought to himself, *no way, you are not going to hurt them, too!*

Kenny grabbed a red rock and started running towards the truck. He ran towards Briggs then confidently fired a shot, hitting Briggs squarely on the shoulder. Briggs fell down, badly injured.

Kenny ran over to the truck to check on his dad and friends. "Dad, you guys okay?" Kenny gasped out.

"Yeah, I'm good dude," said Frank.

"Me, too," answered Paul.

Kenny could see his dad struggling to move in the driver's seat. His dad was pinned.

"Guys, my dad's pinned," said Kenny.

Frank and Paul started getting out of the back of the truck.

"Kenny, I'm okay," said his dad.

Frank said, "We gotta call 911."

Kenny's dad said, "I got it dialed already, Frank. You guys go get that stick from Briggs. I'll be fine."

Kenny paused, wondering about his dad, then asked, "Did you get the evil stone box?"

"Dude, relax, we got it. It was heavy, but we used something to load it into the truck," said Frank.

"Okay then, now we need to get the stick away from Briggs. Right, Kenny?" said Paul.

"Swell," said Frank. "Like that's going to be easy."

Kenny looked back at Briggs. He was holding his badly burned shoulder, but it didn't look like he was going to let it stop him. He had gotten up and was looking at the truck. His face was pure rage.

"Guys, I will draw Briggs away from the truck," said Kenny.

Kenny then ran around the truck and turned to go

down the street, hoping Briggs would follow.

Briggs looked back and forth between Kenny and the truck. As Briggs was deciding which to attack, he caught sight of the evil stone box in the back of the truck.

Briggs looked really puzzled and distracted by the stone box. He seemed almost concerned it was here. He turned to see Kenny at the end of the block. After one more look back at the box, Briggs turned away from the truck and went after Kenny.

Kenny was tired but he knew he had to keep Briggs away from his dad's truck.

Paul was standing next to Frank.

Paul turned and said, "We have to help Kenny."

"I know dude, Briggs is going to mess him up," answered Frank.

But Paul wasn't sure what to do.

As they were trying to decide what to do, there were more screeching tires.

"Ryan!" screamed out Paul.

Ryan had reached the casino but found that the Storyteller had already left.

Paul looked inside Ryan's truck and was glad to see Kenny's other brother, Tommy. He knew they'd need all the help they could get!

"Paul, Frank, hop in,' said Ryan, who was already taking his foot off the brake.

"We gotta help Kenny! Briggs is right on his ass!" yelled Tommy.

Tommy then noticed his dad's truck was smashed.

"Wait, Ryan! Dad's hurt. We gotta help him!" said Tommy.

Frank hopped in and said, "Dude, he's okay. He's on the phone with 911 right now," said Frank.

"We can't wait, Tommy. We gotta help Kenny now," insisted Paul.

Paul jumped in back, pointing. "Let's go, Ryan! He ran around the corner to the right."

Ryan took off toward the corner and turned right. As they rounded the corner, everyone was looking for Kenny and Briggs.

It wasn't hard to see them. Briggs was throwing shots at Kenny, who was dodging back and forth, trying not to get hit.

Ryan kept driving towards Briggs. "If we can get between Briggs and Kenny, we can stop him," said Ryan.

"Ryan, this guy is strong and he can jump some pretty far distances. He caught us earlier and we were going 40," said Paul. "He's possessed right now."

"Paul, no one can run 40 miles per hour. No one can skate 40. You're nuts! He's a big guy, we know that. We have the numbers! We can take him."

Just then Briggs threw another rock at Kenny, and BOOM another car exploded.

Ryan was forced to take a hard left.

"Whoa those fireball things are powerful," said Ryan.

Kenny needed to figure out a way to fight back. He needed to think while simultaneously zigging and zagging away from the constant barrage of fireballs. He needed to think up a distraction to slow down Briggs. He needed time to load rocks into his own stick.

He just wished for a few moments to calm his mind and find a solution. But he was simply, mindlessly running from Briggs. Then he had a thought.

Kenny rounded the next corner then went right down, hiding behind a parked car. He slowed his breathing as best he could and grabbed a red rock and placed it in the stick. He had his moment of calm and he made good use of it.

Briggs came fast around the corner and quickly ran by the parked cars. Kenny popped up just as Briggs realized that Kenny had not kept running.

Kenny shot right at Briggs, who ducked. The shot hit

the wall behind Briggs blowing a hole in it. The force sent Briggs hard into the ground. Kenny loaded up again and moved quickly towards Briggs.

Briggs struggled to get up, but could only prop himself on an elbow. Kenny had definitely shaken him up.

Kenny stood there trying to catch his breath, watching Briggs trying to crawl away. His mind was working fast now, thinking, *how can I get him to let go of the stick?* Then it hit him. *I need to hit his hands. He can't hold the stick if he can't grip the stick!*

Kenny slowly walked to the middle of the street in front of Briggs, who had staggered to his feet.

Kenny shot right at the lower part of the evil stick. The shot flew right at Briggs, but he jumped straight up in the air to get out of the way.

Just then Ryan came around the corner in his truck, and they saw Briggs in the air over Kenny. Ryan couldn't believe how high Briggs was. He saw Kenny and drove straight towards him.

Briggs landed on top of a car parked next to Kenny at the same moment that Ryan pulled up. Paul reached out his hand and pulled Kenny into the back of the truck.

Ryan sped off around the corner. Briggs was furious,

howling as he followed them.

But Briggs did not follow for long. Instead, he stopped and looked around at where he was. He noticed he was standing in front of the police station. Where he had been held when he was arrested.

"What's he doing, Kenny?" asked Paul.

"I don't know. He doesn't seem interested in chasing us anymore," observed Kenny, who was both confused and happy at this turn of events.

Kenny tapped on the window and motioned for Ryan to pull over.

Ryan did so and jumped out. "What the heck is going on?" He was upset about not being able to correlate what he was seeing with what made any sense to him at all.

"Briggs stopped. He's not following us," said Kenny.

"What does he want? Think he's getting low on those rocket rocks?" said Paul.

Kenny looked down at his own bag of red rocks. It was about half full. How many had Briggs shot?

They watched Briggs load a rock. After the rock caught fire in the evil stick Briggs threw it at the police station. He loaded another one, then another. Briggs was showing his anger. The fireballs blew out windows in the police station and started a fire inside.

Kenny remembered that the evil stick wants destruction.

Suddenly Kenny understood, "He wants the town to burn! He doesn't want us, he wants to destroy the town. He wants his revenge on the people who sent him to prison!"

"We have to stop him," said Kenny, "We have to get the stick from him. If we can get the stick from him, we can end it."

"But how do we get the stick from him? We can't get close enough," asked Ryan.

"Leave that part to me," said Kenny. "I will hit his hands and get him to drop it. I need you to stop him, hold him down. He should not be as strong without his stick."

Ryan stared at Kenny in shock. "You want me to do what?" he said in disbelief. "There's no way..."

Kenny loaded a red rock and started walking towards Briggs.

Briggs moved away from the police station and now focused on the stores. His shots caused explosions and started fires in the stores. The people of Brenton had starting coming out to watch what was going on. Police, fire, and many others had come to the spot where Kenny, family, and friends were watching.

They watched as Briggs threw flaming rocks into the businesses on Main Street.

The crowd pointed and talked as they watched the young man approach the huge man.

Kenny had moved in close to Briggs, who was unaware. Kenny took a slow, calm shot, aiming directly at Briggs' lower hand.

BAM! Briggs felt the burn of the hot rock as it hit his right hand then slammed into his side causing his clothing to catch fire.

"AAAHHH!" Briggs let out a painful scream as he went down.

Kenny placed another rock into the stick and stepped even closer to Briggs.

Ryan, Tommy, Paul and Frank had grabbed hockey sticks out of Ryan's truck and had reached Kenny, sticks raised.

"We can take him now," said Ryan menacingly.

"NO!" said Kenny, "He still has the stick in his left hand. He still has the evil power."

Ryan ignored him and ran towards Briggs, who was getting up.

"NO!" yelled Kenny again.

Kenny's yell made Briggs look right at Ryan, who swung his hockey stick right towards Briggs head. But Briggs ducked, deflected Ryan's blow, and hit Ryan with the evil stick.

Ryan flew back and rolled over the top of a nearby car.

"RYAN!" yelled Kenny and Tommy together.

There was no answer. Before Kenny could act, Paul, Frank, and Tommy were running at Briggs.

"You're not doing that to my brother!" yelled Tommy. The three attacked Briggs. And while he fought them off, the diversion bought Kenny some time.

Kenny noticed that the pack Briggs had been carrying with the red rocks was now in the middle of the street. Kenny ran to it, grabbed the bag, and threw it out of sight behind a car.

Kenny yelled out. "He's out of rocks! And his right hand is hurt."

Kenny watched as players from Ryan's clinic and other kids were coming with their hockey sticks.

Briggs began to realize that no one seemed scared of him anymore.

Ryan started to get up from behind the car. He nodded at Kenny that he was ok.

Frank, Tommy, and Paul led the kids as they surrounded Briggs. Briggs backed up slowly, waiting for someone to attack him so he could hurt them and show them they should still be afraid.

But the group just moved Briggs back and back, towards a corner. Briggs had his back to the wall and was surrounded by kids with hockey sticks.

Kenny walked up. He was armed with another fireball.

"Frank, Paul, Tommy! After I hit his left hand he will drop the stick. DO NOT touch the stick. DO NOT let ANYONE touch the stick. Then you need to keep Briggs down. Don't hurt him. Just hold him down."

Kenny walked between the kids to the front, facing Briggs. Briggs stared at Kenny. Kenny looked around at the kids. Briggs was not moving, but he was keenly aware of everyone. He was waiting for something to happen. Briggs was holding the evil stick in his left hand. His right hand was badly burned and bleeding.

Kenny locked his eyes on Briggs' left hand, and under his breath said, "Sorry, I need to do this."

Kenny threw his shot right at Briggs. They were so close that Briggs had no time to react, and the rock slammed into his left hand. Briggs dropped the stick and fell to the ground in incredible pain.

Kenny yelled out, "Nobody touch the stick! Don't touch the stick!"

Tommy reacted first and reached Briggs, tackling him to pin him to the ground. Frank and Paul jumped on to hold him down.

Briggs tried to fight them off. Tommy struggled to hold on and fell off. But Frank and Paul held on, and Tommy jumped back on. They had them.

Kenny ran over to protect the stick from anyone touching it, putting himself between it and the growing crowd. Just as he did so, the crowd parted and White Crane appeared. He had two pieces of wood that had notches in them.

White Crane asked, "Where is the stone box?"

"We have it. It's in the truck," answered Kenny.

White Crane smiled, "Excellent. We must move quickly."

He handed Kenny one of the shafts of wood.

"Slide this under that end of the evil stick and we will walk this over to the stone box."

White Crane turned to Frank, Tommy, and Paul who were holding down Briggs.

"Do not let him up until we are done," he commanded.

With that, White Crane bent down and Kenny followed his lead. They picked up the evil stick using the wooden paddles.

"Kenny, these paddles have been handed down in our family of Storytellers. They have special powers to prevent the evil from transferring to us."

They walked the stick over to the truck. An ambulance had arrived and the paramedics had already freed Cody from the crushed truck.

With the utmost concentration, White Crane and Kenny placed the evil stick back into the evil stone box. White Crane motioned to Kenny to close the lid. Kenny did as instructed. The box made a loud crackling noise, followed by a hiss.

As soon as the hiss subsided, there was an immediate change in Briggs. He stopped struggling against the boys and instead acted like a man in severe pain. He was confused and disoriented, and did not know where he was.

The boys got off him and called for help.

Kenny frantically motioned at the ambulance to follow him over to Briggs. They arrived to find Briggs in severe pain and the crowd trying to comfort him. Everyone seemed to understand that the evil was in the stick and no longer in Briggs.

Briggs was loaded into the ambulance, and taken to the hospital. As the ambulance drove off, Kenny went back over to his dad's truck. The stone box was being loaded into the limousine. White Crane was standing nearby, waiting for Kenny.

"What will you do with it?" asked Kenny as he watched the box disappear into the limousine.

"It will be hidden from all of us. We need to protect it from ourselves. You cannot know where it is."

Kenny nodded in agreement, and relief. The limousine drove away and he felt like the weight of the world had just lifted from his shoulders.

Ryan pulled up in his truck.

Kenny shook himself with a sudden realization and said, "Casey! Where is Casey."

"It's okay. I just talked to mom. Casey and dad are okay, and at the hospital. Let's go see 'em."

Kenny smiled and hopped into the truck with his brothers and friends.

20

White Crane

Kenny walked into the hospital room and saw his dad and Casey sitting up and talking away. There were stories to tell now. He gave both a hug and sat between them.

Casey smiled, "So? How does it feel to be the town hero?"

Kenny only smiled.

"Hey, maybe your dad will let you play lacrosse now," she said, winking at Kenny.

Cody looked over, "Now don't go getting carried

away with this lacrosse stuff. You're going to need some teammates."

Ryan pointed to the TV in their room.

"Check it out, dad. They have professional lacrosse. I guess we have a team. They're called the Swarm. The Minnesota Swarm. Who knew?"

Everyone in the room laughed.

Casey looked over at Kenny, "What happened to the evil stick?"

Kenny looked at her and said, "Well, the Storyteller took the stick. He felt no one should know where it is. I think he's right. We probably shouldn't go looking for it."

Casey chuckled in agreement then added, "I wonder where he is going to hide it? How will we know it's safe?"

Kenny was thinking the same thing, too. "I don't know. I guess we have to trust him to do the right thing," he said. "Maybe we should go see him when you're out of the hospital."

Ryan interrupted, "Kenny, I told dad they have lacrosse over the 'U'".

Kenny perked up, "The Gophers have a lacrosse team?"

Ryan answered, "Yah, it's club right now, but I thought I might try it. It looks like fun. We've been watching highlights on YouTube. Those Frost guys you told us about seem to have some fun with it."

Kenny's mom said, "We've been talking to some others who have stopped by. There is a youth lacrosse program down in the Cities. Grand Rapids has some teams and we were thinking maybe you'd like to start a youth league next spring for Brenton."

Kenny's face lit up with excitement.

"Really? Would you really do that?"

"But you're gonna have to teach us the game and some skills. And you can't use that stick, ok?" teased Casey. "It's not fair against the rest of us."

"Don't worry, dad told me he was gonna buy me a real stick. Right, dad?" said Kenny.

"When did I say that?" asked Cody.

"Remember? At your office after I met the Frost guys?" answered Kenny, smiling back.

Casey then asked, "What happened to Briggs? Where is he?"

The group all went quiet.

Kenny's mom answered, "I talked to the doctors and he was burned pretty badly on his hands and legs. He broke his right shoulder, too. But they say he should heal up in a few months. It's going to be a tough recovery."

Kenny turned to his dad. "Dad, you going to hire him back?"

Cody smiled and looked over, saying, "Who said I fired him?"

Kenny looked at Casey, "So, when are they gonna let you out of here?"

Casey held up her left arm to show the cast on her wrist. "Not long, they just wanted me here for a little while for the asphalt face plant. Make sure I don't have a serious concussion."

"How about the leg?" asked Kenny.

"Oh it's just a hairline fracture, don't even need a cast," she answered.

A few weeks passed and Casey got her cast off. Kenny got a real lacrosse stick. Dad also bought sticks for Frank, Paul, and Casey.

One Saturday afternoon in September they were throwing and catching at the park. Each were trying new tricks and learning how to shoot with the same accuracy they had in hockey.

Frank called out, "Watch this dudes!" as he shot.

He hit the hockey net top right corner. "That's how you put the rock in the box!" Frank exclaimed.

Just then a white limousine pulled up. The bright white color of the limousine looked amazing on the fall day with the orange and red colors of the trees.

They all stopped playing and walked toward the limo. To their surprise, Ron got of out the limousine first, followed by a few of his friends. Kenny and Casey recognized them from the cave when they were trapped.

They stopped moving towards the limousine now and looked quite hesitant as one more person got out. It was White Crane, the one they had been expecting.

White Crane walked over to Kenny and his friends. Kenny was thinking, *does he want the stick back? What is going on?* He felt very uneasy with Ron and his friends there. But he trusted White Crane, so he was waiting for an explanation.

White Crane approached and smiled, "Kenny. Casey. Hello my friends. How are you doing?"

Kenny answered for the group, "We are fine, White Crane. Why are you here, and with them?" He'd tried to sound casual, but he knew it sounded...accusatory.

White Crane said, "I have been talking with our Nation and discussing the return of the sticks. We see it as

223

a sign, and there is action to be taken."

Casey stepped forward. "What kind of action are you planning to take?"

White Crane smiled. "Relax, everyone. Ron and his friends are here with me to offer an idea. The stick represents something very special to us. We started thinking and realized our Nation has not been taught nor played the game for generations. We think it would be a good time to return the game to our children, and teach them to play lacrosse again."

Kenny and the others looked at each other.

"We were talking about creating a lacrosse league here in Brenton. Do you want to join us?" asked Kenny.

White Crane looked at Ron and turned back to Kenny. "We thank you for your offer, but we would like to form our own teams. We would have our own teams and you could have your own teams. You could come and play against us. Then at special events we can show off the sticks."

"Sticks?" answered Kenny in sudden alarm. "I thought you hid the evil stick so no one would find it?"

"Kenny, that stick is indeed hidden. I am talking about another stick," said White Crane.

White Crane started walking back to the limousine.

Kenny and the others followed in deep curiosity.

Kenny whispered to Casey, "Did he find another one?"

Casey shrugged, "Maybe. Ron?"

They followed White Crane to the back of the limousine. The driver opened the trunk, and there was a beautiful white case. The case was the size of a lacrosse stick and it had beautiful white trim with white feathers.

The driver lifted the case and held it in his arms. He reached over and opened the latch. They all watched as the case slowly opened and revealed the pearl-white shaft of a lacrosse stick. The stick was completely white. The shaft end rolled into an amazing knob in the shape of a cranes beak. The head was long and skinny, shaped like the white head of a bird.

White Crane pulled out the stick and held it. The stick started glowing a beautiful pearl white. Kenny and the group stared in awe at the Flamethrower stick.

Kenny asked, "Where did you get that? Where did you find that one?"

White Crane moved the stick around to show how it shined and its wonderful glow when he held it.

"I was given this by my father. It was his. After my great grandfather buried his stick he showed his son where it was. That way when the Creator changed his mind and allowed the Flamethrowers to come back, he would know exactly where it was."

"This was not allowed by the Creator, but the location was passed down to my father. One day he heard the call of the stick, much like you did. He found the stone box and opened it. He never located the red rocks as you did. I was unsure if that part of the story was real until you came back with them." White Crane looked gratefully at Kenny, who was smiling with pride.

White Crane continued, "My father decided that since no other sticks had been found, it was better not to reveal it. He showed me the stick a few times when I was growing up. After he died the stick became mine."

Kenny asked, "How many other sticks are there?"

"Remember," answered White Crane, "There was one given to each Nation. So there was one Flamethrower for each first Nation."

"But how many Nations were there?" asked Casey.

"We do not know for sure. In the beginning there were many Nations, but after the Nations lost many people, they joined together. I suppose each animal was represented in the beginning by the Creator."

"So, like, where do you think the other sticks are?" asked Paul.

"I have wondered the same thing myself," answered White Crane. "But I do not know. What I do know is the story says that when one is revealed they all shall be revealed."

White Crane turned to Kenny and said solemnly, "Kenny, others will be found now."

"Dude," said Frank, "What other cool sticks have you heard about?"

"Ah, Frank," said White Crane. "I expected you would ask that. There are many sticks I have heard stories about. The Bison and Polar Bear were long sticks and very strong. I have heard stories about the Wolverine and Wolf sticks. The Scorpion is a special orange stick with the ability to shoot from either end. The Great Fish stick and Snake stick are smooth and flexible. The Toad stick is supposed to be the most beautiful, with many brilliant colors."

A red tail hawk appeared above them. The hawk was squawking loudly as if to gain the attention of the people below. White Crane stepped away from the group and held his stick out high. The hawk swooped down and landed on the stick.

White Crane acted as if the hawk was an old friend, telling him a story. He listened intently.

The hawk then looked at Kenny, turned, and flew upwards towards the blue sky.

White Crane walked back over to Kenny.

"The polar bear stick has been found," said White Crane.

"You were right," said Kenny, in a daze.

"It is a long stick, some say over 7 feet long, with a light blue shaft like ice," said White Crane.

The group of friends looked at each other as if to say *what now ?*

White Crane turned to Kenny. "Kenny, we need to go."

About the Author

J. Alan Childs was born and raised in the San Fernando Valley, in Southern California. He was taught a passion for hockey by the "Cahill gang", David, Danny, Kevin, Brian, and others. He moved to Minnesota to raise his family with a hockey tradition. Turns out all five kids developed a passion for lacrosse. Who knew?

Alan currently resides in Savage, Minnesota with his wife, five kids, two dogs, two cats, and Harry, the hedgehog. He serves as the Commissioner for Burnsville Lacrosse and Vice President of the Youth Lacrosse of Minnesota (YLM). He can be found in local rinks and fields filming his kids playing hockey and lacrosse.

Made in the USA
Lexington, KY
12 March 2013